Shopper's Checklist

After you finish reading this book, fill out this card and bring it with you when you're shopping for a computer. Use it to jog your memory, or simply hand it to the salesperson and say, "What've you got that matches these specs?"

Kinds of application programs you'll be using:

❏ Word processing ❏ Spreadsheets ❏ Database
❏ Business graphics ❏ Graphic arts ❏ Desktop publishing
❏ Educational ❏ Games

Where you'll be using the computer: ❏ Home ❏ Office

Will this computer be part of a network? ❏ Yes ❏ No

What kind of pages do you need to print?

❏ Draft-quality text and graphics ❏ Letter-quality text
❏ Text and graphics ❏ Color

Special things I need my computer to do:

_____

_____

Describe the CPU You Want:

Preferred microprocessor:

PC: ❏ 80386 ❏ 80486SX ❏ 80486
Macintosh: ❏ 68020 ❏ 68030 ❏ 68040

How fast (in megahertz)?

❏ 16 ❏ 20 ❏ 25 ❏ 33 ❏ 50 ❏ 66

(50 and 66 only available to 486 computers)

How much memory (RAM)?

❏ 2 megabytes ❏ 4 megabytes ❏ 8 megabytes ❏ More! (specify) _____

How big a hard disk?

❏ 80 megabytes ❏ 120 megabytes ❏ 224 megabytes ❏ 340 megabytes

Which size floppy disk drives (PC-compatibles only, you may need both sizes)?

❏ 5¼-inch ❏ 3½-inch

(Make sure you get high density, regardless of the size.)

Describe the Monitor You Want:

❏ Black-and-white
❏ Grayscale
　　How many grays? ❏ 16 ❏ 64 ❏ 256
❏ Color
　　How many colors? ❏ 16 ❏ 256 ❏ 16 million

What size screen?

❏ Normal (12–15-inch) ❏ Full-page ❏ Double-page

Monitor notes:

_____

Describe Your Computer's Input/Output Needs

What kind of keyboard?

PC-compatible: ❏ 101-key   ❏ More! (specify) _____

Macintosh   ❏ Normal   ❏ Extended

What kind of mouse (PC-compatibles only)?

❏ Serial mouse   ❏ Bus mouse

Which communication ports, and how many (PC-compatibles only)?

❏ Serial   ❏ One   ❏ Two   ❏ More! (specify) _____

❏ Parallel   ❏ One   ❏ Two

❏ SCSI

❏ Network (specify which kind) _____

Input/output notes:

_____

_____

What Options Do You Want?

Speed enhancements:

❏ Doubled clock speed   ❏ Hard disk cache   ❏ Match coprocessor

❏ Local-bus video   ❏ Graphics coprocessor   ❏ Shadow RAM

Peripherals you intend to use (now or in the future):

❏ Modem

❏ Fax modem

Scanner: ❏ Grayscale   ❏ Color   ❏ Slide scanner   ❏ Video

Mass storage: ❏ Cartridge drive   ❏ Second hard disk   ❏ Tape backup   ❏ CD drive

Kind of printer you intend to use:

❏ Dot-matrix   ❏ 9-pin   ❏ 24-pin

❏ Laser or laser-like printer   ❏ 300 dots per inch   ❏ More! (specify)_____

❏ Inkjet

❏ Color   ❏ Dot-matrix   ❏ Inkjet   ❏ Thermal transfer

Options notes:

_____

_____

Important Questions To Ask

▼ Will your dealer provide the warranty service? Do they have a repair department?

▼ Is your dealer an authorized dealer for the make of computer you're buying?

▼ What's covered by the warranty?

▼ Will the dealer pre-configure the computer so that it's ready to use?

▼ Will the dealer include the operating system software in the deal?

▼ Is training or after-sale technical support available?

I HATE

BUYING A COMPUTER

JIM FELICI

I Hate Buying a Computer

Copyright © 1993 by Que® Corporation

Library of Congress Catalog No.: 93-60610

ISBN: 1-56529-278-2

95 94 93   6 5 4 3 2 1

Interpretation of the printing code: the rightmost double-digit number is the year of the book's printing; the rightmost single-digit number, the number of the book's printing. For example, a printing code of 93-1 shows that the first printing of the book occurred in 1993.

Screen reproductions in this book were created using Collage Plus from Inner Media, Inc., Hollis, NH.

Shoe®&©, 1993, Tribune Media Services, Inc. All Rights Reserved.

Publisher: David P. Ewing

Associate Publisher: Rick Ranucci

Publishing Plan Manager: Thomas H. Bennett

Acquisitions Editor: Sarah Browning

Dedication

To Esther and Walter Felici, a.k.a. Mom and Pop, who taught their kid how to talk straight, even if he doesn't think that way all the time.

About the Author

As a kid, **Jim Felici** thought about being a scientist. But differential calculus convinced him that the liberal arts might be a better idea. Turning to journalism, he became addicted to seeing his name in print and pursued a career in publishing. He could see no reason for polluting his life with computers until he found out you could use them to set type—including his own byline. In short order he was writing and editing for leading computer magazines, including *PC World* and *Macworld*. Eventually, he became Technical Editor and Managing Editor of *Publish* magazine.

Felici (only his relatives call him Jim, or James if they're mad at him) has bought enough computers in his day for both personal and business use to get over his loathing for computer shopping. Tragically, his first computer was obsolete within weeks of its purchase, which scarred him for life and taught him that man must not shop by price alone.

Currently, Felici owns a Gateway 2000 4DX2-66V 80486 PC-compatible and an Apple Macintosh IIcx 68030, and he loves and hates them equally in turns. Having worked with PCs since they shipped with 128K of memory and with Macintoshes before the world even knew they existed, he knows both machines all too well.

After agonizing years of learning about computers, he's realized that 90% of what he's taken in has no practical value whatsoever. Most of the other 10% is in this book.

Credits

Title Manager:
Shelley O'Hara

Product Development Specialist:
Elden Nelson

Production Editor:
Heather Northrup

Editors:
Barbara K. Koenig
Cindy Morrow

Technical Editor:
Bruce Meyer

Novice Reviewer:
Paul Marchesseault

Editorial Assistants:
Julia Blount
Sandra Naito

Production Team:
Danielle Bird
Julie Brown
Paula Carroll
Michelle Greenwalt
Bob LaRoche
Caroline Roop
Linda Seifert
Sandra Shay
Amy Steed
Tina Trettin
Michelle Worthington
Lillian Yates

Indexer:
Joy Dean Lee

Cover Illustration by Jeff MacNelly.

Composed in *Goudy* and *MCPdigital* by Que Corporation.

Acknowledgments

I should thank the deranged computer marketers who have muddied the waters so well that they've created a wide open market for this book. But I prefer to thank Jennifer Griffith for keeping me on my editorial rails, critiquing the text, and warning me when the fog started getting too thick. She also persistently helped me out of my "I Hate Writing Computer Books" spells. Thanks, sweetie.

Trademark Acknowledgments

All terms mentioned in this book that are known to be trademarks or service marks have been appropriately capitalized. Que cannot attest to the accuracy of this information. Use of a term in this book should not be regarded as affecting the validity of any trademark or service mark.

Contents at a Glance

Table of Contents

Introduction

Panic.

Uncontrollable shaking.

Sheer dread.

Do these symptoms sound familiar? If so, you must be suffering from one of the two most frightening experiences modern people endure. Either it's tax time, or you've just walked into your local Computers R Us store.

Shopping for a computer can be scary. Mysterious words and numbers jump out from every corner. Salespeople turn up their noses at you if you don't know their confusing terms. ("What? You don't know what a *Borgenflotcher Overdrive* is?") Finally, computers all look so much *alike*—how are you supposed to tell which is the right one to get?

Free truth is, buying a computer doesn't have to be that hard. Once you get past all the confusing technobabble and advertising hype, it's a lot like buying a very expensive kitchen appliance. This book helps you learn the absolute essentials so you can find a machine that does what you need.

This book won't try to teach you everything there is to know about computers. (Trust me, you don't want to know.) Instead, you'll get right to the meat of things. You'll learn what types of computers are used and what your computer needs to work well. Then you can get to work, leaving the obscure stuff to people who don't have better things to do.

What about Those Drawings in the Margin?

All the information in this book is *not* created equal. Occasionally, the book includes something more technical than the rest. This book uses icons (those funny drawings within the margins) to say things like "Hey, this is technical. You don't have to read it." The book has other icons that tell you when to be careful, alert you to some frustrating aspect of computers you'll have to deal with, and so on.

Here are the icons and what they mean.

"I HATE THIS!"

This icon tells you when the book has to explain something frustrating or confusing. It's a good idea to read the text next to this icon; it'll help you brace yourself for things to come.

TIP

You'll see this icon next to shortcuts, tricks, and time-savers—things you can use to make your life easier.

EXPERTS ONLY

If you're in the mood to read more detailed information on something, seek out this icon. This is interesting, useful stuff, but it's more advanced, and you don't have to know it to buy your computer.

BUZZWORDS

BUZZWORDS

Computer people have made up hundreds of new words. This picture alerts you that one of these mysterious terms is about to be explained.

CAUTION

This icon says, "Watch out!" The information next to it can help you avoid common pitfalls.

PART I

The Lay of the Land

Includes:

CHAPTER 1

Don't Panic!

IN A NUTSHELL

- ▼ Why you shouldn't be afraid of computers
- ▼ Decide what you'll use the computer for
- ▼ Get acquainted with what's out there
- ▼ Stick to your budget

Computers are complicated beasts, but you don't need to study computer programming and engineering at MIT to buy or use one. After all, most of the gadgets you keep around the house are far too complicated to completely understand, but you can still buy and use them. For instance, the principles of electrical conduction and resistance are complicated … but that doesn't stop you from using your toaster.

It's not technology that makes buying a computer a chore—it's all the marketing static that goes along with it. There are so many choices, so many prices, and so many weird words that get tossed around.

Before paralysis sets in, you must cut the task down to size. This chapter gives you the first five steps to get you going on what could otherwise be a pretty frightening journey. Don't worry, though. With this book, it'll be easy.

Step 1: Repeat after Me: "I Am *Not* Scared by Technology!"

We've been taught that computers are talismans of mighty science and that scientists are like high priests, to be venerated and held in awe. Those initiated into the rites of the computer cult, therefore, inherit this mantle of wisdom.

Nothing is farther from the truth. There are just as many dopes sitting at the keyboards of computers as there are sitting at the wheels of cars, the keyboards of cash registers, or in the padded seats of various local, state, and federal governments.

I HATE BUYING A COMPUTER!

To buy a computer, you need to know less about one than you need to know about a car when you buy one. The big difference is that cars are familiar and computers aren't.

TIP

When buying a computer, if you hear a word or concept you don't understand, demand an immediate explanation. Never, never, never be embarrassed to ask. Generally, the reason you're not understanding is that something is being badly explained. And don't be bashful about following up the explanation with the question, "And why is that important?"

Step 2: Decide What You're Going To Do with the Computer

If you want the right tool for the job, it helps to know what the job is first. The more specific you can be about this job, the better. If you know people who use computers in a way that you'd like to, ask them about their work and the way they use their computers. The best way to learn is from people who share your interests. Ask them what kind of computers they bought and why. They may have some pretty good suggestions (but then again, maybe they just got sucked in by some fast-talking salesperson, so don't take their word as gospel).

You should also think about what you might want to do with the machine two or three years down the road. As you realize what a useful tool a computer can be, you may expand your ideas about how to use it. You want a machine that can accommodate your grand scheme for the future.

I HATE BUYING A COMPUTER!

▼ **Word Processor**: The computer has definitely replaced the type-writer as the writing tool of choice. With a word-processing program, you can easily create and revise documents.

▼ **Spreadsheet:** If you're the accounting, economical, or just plain organized type, you're probably thinking about using your computer to perform calculations. Spreadsheet programs do this sort of thing beautifully.

▼ **Database:** This is one of the scariest terms in computerdom, but it's really pretty simple. If you want to collect and organize large amounts of information on any topic, you're thinking of using your computer for a database.

▼ **Publishing:** Maybe you have the task of producing a company newsletter, and you want your computer to be your press. Desktop publishing and design programs can help you make that company newsletter look really professional.

▼ **Games:** Hey, you've got to take time out for fun, haven't you?

CAUTION

A computer is just a tool, and if you don't have a job for it, you won't use it. If you're thinking about buying a computer just because you feel you should own one, chances are good that it'll end up in the basement next to the exercise bike.

HARDWARE and SOFTWARE

The *hardware* of a computer is its tangible parts: the keyboard, the monitor, and so forth. Logical enough. But then some wise guy decided that a cute name for computer programs would be *software*. Unfortunately, the name stuck. Software is also called *programs* and *applications*.

Step 3: Buy the Biggest, Fattest Computer Magazine You Can Find

A computer magazine is a great way to learn about how computers are promoted and to get an overview of the market. Skip the articles; they're probably boring anyway. Set your magazine down on a sturdy table, and just look at the computer ads (save the other ads for later). Get a sense of what things cost. Note how the machines are discussed and compared, even if you don't know exactly what the ads are talking about most of the time. Looking at ads is a great way to do some initial research on your own terms, without having to deal with salespeople.

Step 4: Read This Book

To understand the practical implications of all the technobabble you see in the magazine (including its articles), just keep reading this book. Your traveler's guide to the foreign language of computer sales is the Buzzwords Glossary in the back of this book. There's a computer culture out

there that likes to speak in tongues, using sinister-sounding code words. After you read this book, you can fight back with snappy put-downs like, "BIOS shadow RAM? I can't be worried about a millisecond here or there!"

"I HATE THIS!"

I don't understand what this salesperson is saying!

It may seem that computer salespeople are deliberately trying to intimidate you with their technical prowess. More likely, they're just trying to sound knowledgeable. But in either case, many aren't very knowledgeable at all. Even among those who are knowledgeable, many only know about the models that are sold in the stores in which they work. These are two very powerful reasons to shop around. You're looking for a good computer and for someone who can accurately represent it to you.

Look for a salesperson who can explain things to you in plain English. Some computerese is unavoidable, but most of the jargon of high-tech can be translated into clear and simple language. When you find a salesperson who can explain things in this way, unload every question you can think of. Remember that one of a salesperson's jobs is to inform and educate. Don't be bashful about using computer salespeople as private computer tutors. Ask them about computers that compete against the ones they sell.

The person with the clearest answers may not have the best prices, but someone helpful and lucid may be very useful if you have questions after you take your computer home.

Step 5: Set a Budget and Stick to It

No matter what you decide to spend, you can get something a little better for just $100 more. Before you know it, your planned $1,000 purchase can balloon int,o a $2,000 investment.

As you shop, stick to your original budget for as long as you can. Don't let anyone talk you up in price until you've had a chance to survey the field. Keep in mind that you always pay less than the list price for a computer—as with stereos, the list price is there just for contrast.

TIP

> When you're buying a computer, don't talk about how much you have to spend—talk about the job you have to do. If you lead with your wallet, your salesperson will always have "just the thing for you." At the outset, at least, have the salesperson propose a computer to fit your task, not your budget.

Computers with equivalent capabilities have similar prices as well. But don't drive yourself crazy looking for absolutely the best deal—you'll never find it. There are too many choices to check out, and prices fluctuate all the time.

Ballpark budgets

▼ If you plan to use your computer mainly for writing and games at home, you should be able to keep your costs under $1,500.

▼ If you need a computer for small business use, expect to spend between $2,000 and $2,500.

continues

I HATE BUYING A COMPUTER!

Ballpark budgets (continued)

▼ If you need a computer to do desktop publishing or fancy design work, you may need to spend as much as $4,000.

▼ Unless you go completely hog-wild, you should never have to spend more than $4,500 on a computer.

"I HATE THIS!"

"I could've paid HOW much less?!"

Two days after you buy your computer, you'll probably find something for a few dollars less advertised somewhere else. That's life. In the computer marketplace, great deals are everywhere, and prices are constantly dropping. Don't let yourself fall into the "I'll just wait for the prices to drop one more time" trap, or you'll find yourself waiting forever and never getting the benefit of having the computer.

CHAPTER 2

The Nuts and Bolts

(Taking the Hard Out of Computer Hardware)

IN A NUTSHELL

- ▼ What hardware and software mean
- ▼ PCs vs. Macintoshes
- ▼ Hardware: three easy pieces
- ▼ Chips, memory, and disks
- ▼ All about monitors

f the big sale at the computer store ends in 15 minutes, and you need to get hip to these machines *now*, this chapter's for you. Here you'll find the lowdown on the major parts of a computer—what they are, what they do, and how to shop for them.

Hardware vs. Software

Computer hardware is like a car. It has the capability to move, but can't do anything on its own. So *hardware* is the computer itself. Computer *software* is like you, the driver of the car. Just like a car needs a driver to go anywhere, computers need software to do anything. Just like learning to drive a car was a little difficult, learning to use software might be a little tricky for you at first.

Depending on what software you're using, your computer can do just about anything. The computer's a chameleon, becoming what the software tells it to be: a word processor for handling text, for example, or an accountant's spreadsheet, an electronic classroom, or a game for whiling away the hours (or days).

Examples of hardware and software

▼ The keyboard—the thing you type on—is hardware.

▼ The monitor—the thing you stare at—is hardware.

▼ The *central processing unit* (CPU), which sounds like an obscure government agency but is the heart of the computer, is hardware.

▼ WordPerfect and Microsoft Word are software. They're the most popular packages to get if you want to use your computer for writing and editing.

▼ Lotus 1-2-3 and Excel are software; they're good packages to get for doing spreadsheets.

▼ Where In the World Is Carmen Sandiego? is software; it's a great game for getting your kids to learn about geography, without realizing you've tricked them into being educated.

"I HATE THIS!"

"If I hear one more acronym, I'm going to scream!"
"This 20-MIPS CPU's ASIC can RIP 10K cps!" Yes, computerphiles can gag you with their acronyms for hardware. Fight back! Put these brazen show-offs in their place by demanding a translation into plain English. The chances are they can't do it.

The Leading Contenders: PCs and Macintoshes

There are only two kinds of personal computers you should consider buying: IBM PC compatibles and Apple Macintoshes. Many people say Macintoshes are easier to use, although that's changing. PCs are cheaper. Because PCs generally cost less, there are a *lot* more of them around. If you plan to eventually share your computer work with other people's computers, the odds favor getting a PC.

But don't reject the Macintosh outright. Recently, Apple Corporation has been aggressively pricing the Macintosh, so they're becoming more popular. Also, you can now buy Macintoshes in regular superstores instead of just the exclusive hoity-toity computer boutiques. To further confuse the issue, you can make Macintoshes run PC-style software, giving you the both of best worlds.

The final analysis? If you work with people who all use a specific type of computer, you'll be best off bending to peer pressure and getting that kind of machine. That way, the work you do on your computer is easily transferable to your friends' computers. Plus, when you have problems, you'll automatically have a support group to get things going again.

BUZZWORDS

CLONE

When IBM introduced its first personal computer (the IBM PC, still a trademark), it became an instant standard, and many companies copied its design. These work-alikes were called PC-compatibles or PC-clones. Today, they're generically called PCs. There are now over 40 major manufacturers of IBM PC-compatible computers selling in the U.S. They account for about 75% of all personal computer sales. When this book refers to a PC, it doesn't necessarily mean IBM; it means any of these compatible computers.

"I HATE THIS!"

Stop this insane bickering!

It can be hard to get a straight opinion about computers. Mac fanatics and PC fanatics sneer at each other and each other's contemptible equipment. Both are nuts. Macs and PCs are both tools that work toward the same end. They get you to stay at your desk until the moon rises, all in the name of increased productivity.

Important differences between Macintoshes and PCs

▼ Some Macintoshes, if set up properly, can use PC software. No PC can use Macintosh software.

▼ There's so much PC software—literally thousands of packages—that most PC owners never give a second's thought to owning Macintosh software.

▼ There are dozens of work-alike PC brands; there are no Macintosh work-alikes. As a result, PC pricing has to be more competitive.

▼ Macs have always been easy to use. PCs are just beginning to be easy to use.

Hardware: Three Easy Pieces

Computers are made up of three parts. You absolutely, positively, without a doubt, *must* have one of each of these in order to use your computer. And all three have to be designed so that they work together. The parts are the following:

▼ **The CPU** (which stands for *central processing unit*). This box contains the guts of the computer. It's where all the computing happens.

▼ **The monitor**. This is the TV-like screen where the computer shows you what it's doing and what your work looks like. Basically, you're just looking for one that doesn't make you bleary-eyed.

▼ **The keyboard**. This is how you feed information into the computer. Because you can do more things with a computer than a typewriter, you get more keys—lots more keys.

TIP

Your best bet is to buy the components of your computer as a matched set, just as you would buy a stereo. You get the best price, and the pieces are guaranteed to work well together. While you're at it, look for a set that includes software too!

The CPU is the most expensive part of the computer because all the magic goes on in there. The monitor just displays pictures, and the keyboard is just a bunch of dumb buttons.

When you talk about buying a computer, then, you're really talking about buying the CPU. The monitor costs extra, but usually not much extra, depending on the size of the screen and how many colors you get.

The keyboard, meanwhile, is so cheap that it's generally thrown in for free. Likewise, you'll usually get a free *mouse*—a little hand-held gizmo that causes a pointer to move around on the monitor's screen when you slide it around on your desktop. You use it for telling programs what to do.

TIP

Many computers are sold with software already installed inside them, which means that you can start working on the computer as soon as you take it out of the box and turn it on. This arrangement saves you time and energy. It also guarantees that someone has gotten your computer to work before you lug it all the way home. Find a computer dealer who will do this for you free of charge.

What Makes the CPU So Expensive?

There's a mess of electronics inside a computer, but when you're buying one, you don't have to worry about most of them. When it comes to the price and capabilities of your computer, your big concerns boil down to these three components, which account for over half the cost of the machine:

▼ The kind of microprocessor the CPU uses as its brain

▼ The amount of information the computer can handle at one time (that is, how much *memory* it has)

▼ How much permanent storage (on recording devices called *disk drives*) the computer provides. This is the computer equivalent of closet space.

BUZZWORDS

MICROPROCESSOR

A microprocessor is a small layered silicon wafer or *chip* containing thousands of transistors. (These transistors are called *semiconductors* to make you think they're somehow better than the things that make your pocket radio work.)

BUZZWORDS

RAM

Computer people in the know (or who want to sound that way) call computer memory RAM. This term stands for *random access memory*, a fact not worth knowing. One talks about "how much RAM" a computer has. If you talk about "how many RAMs" your computer has, you will have irretrievably blown your veneer of hipness.

I HATE BUYING A COMPUTER!

Chips?!! I Have To Know About Chips?!!

Don't worry. Various models of computers are identified by the micro-processor they use. It's like identifying the power of a car by how many cylinders its engine has. Who cares what a cylinder is—but you know that a car with eight of them is more powerful than a car with only four.

Chips are identified by number, and these numbers are logically ar-ranged. The higher the number is, the faster and more powerful the computer is that uses it. PCs and Macintoshes use different chips. Here's the lowdown on the main numbers to know:

IBM PC-compatibles:

Chip Name	Description
8086, 8088, 80286	All different, but all out-of-date. Avoid them.
80386	Cheap and fast enough for almost any work
80486	Expensive and very fast, for pros and macho types

Apple Macintoshes:

Chip Name	Description
68000	It's history. Avoid it.
68020	The minimum, too slow for high-power programs

Chip Name	Description
68030	The best marriage of speed and economy
68040	Way fast, the choice of the demanding and the boastful

Thanks for the Memory

A computer needs memory to perform its brainwork. When you buy a computer, you have to decide how much memory your computer needs. But exactly what is this memory, anyway?

A computer's microprocessor is like a mathematician at a blackboard who writes equations, discovers solutions, and then erases the blackboard to start the next calculation. For its blackboards, the computer uses electronic memory chips. And just as bigger blackboards allow the mathematician to do more elaborate equations, more memory allows computers to perform more complex calculations.

In other words, the computer does its "thinking" in memory, and the more memory it has; the more efficiently it can think.

CAUTION

Memory is short-term storage. When you turn off your computer or trip over the power cord, the electricity to the memory chips is cut off, and everything that was stored there disappears. Poof! To avoid the heartbreak of Poof!, you have to save your work on some sort of disk. You'll learn about disks and disk drives in just a moment, so hold yer horses.

I HATE BUYING A COMPUTER!

BUZZWORDS

MEGABYTE

Computer memory is measured in megabytes (M). A mega-byte is a million bytes. And a byte is a measure of computer information, like a teaspoon or a gram. One typed letter takes up one byte. A megabyte, then, is enough memory to hold about three books the size of this one.

How Much Memory Is Enough?

The minimum these days on any computer is 2 megabytes. Some programs run perfectly well on only 1 megabyte, but there are fewer and fewer such programs around. A machine with 4 or more megabytes is worthwhile insurance against memory-hog programs.

Clever computer programmers keep writing programs that need more and more memory. What's enough this year won't be in a couple of years. But don't fret; you can add more memory later, and it's pretty cheap (and getting cheaper). If you decide later on that you want to add memory, it will cost you in the neighborhood of $70 a megabyte. Installation takes less than five minutes, so even if you hire someone to do it for you, it should be very cheap.

CAUTION

Most software packages list minimum memory requirements on the outside of the box. For instance, they'll say "This program needs a minimum of 1M of RAM." That may be true, but often it's like saying "All you need to cross the Atlantic is an inner tube." Technically true, but kind of misleading. Look instead for a program manufacturer's recommended amount of memory.

Disks: the Hard and the Floppy

Built into the CPU are storage devices—electronic filing cabinets—called disk drives, where your computer stores the software you use, as well as all the documents, pictures, and other files you create on the computer. Until you save your work on a disk, it's floating vulnerably in memory.

Hard disks are permanently mounted inside the computer. Computers typically have one hard disk, which holds all the software and work you use with your computer.

Computers also need a floppy disk drive so that you can copy your software to your hard disk drive, as well as share information with other computers.

Hard disks hold much more information than floppy disks—think of a hard disk as your main filing cabinet. You use floppy disks mostly for moving information around—the same way you might use a briefcase.

Fun Disk Factoids

▼ Floppy disks come in two sizes—3 1/2-inch wide and 5 1/4-inch wide. PCs can use both sizes. Macintoshes can only use the smaller ones.

▼ If you're buying a PC, it's good (but not necessary) to have both a 5 1/4-inch and a 3 1/2-inch floppy disk drive because you never know which size disk you may need to use.

▼ You definitely need a hard disk. No conscientious computer salesperson would sell you a computer without a hard disk.

continues

▼ Different hard disks can hold different amounts of information. Don't buy one that holds less than 80 megabytes, or you'll fill it up in no time. You'll be happier with one that holds at least 120 megabytes. If your wallet is just stuffed with cash, you may want to go up to 200 megabytes.

▼ 200 megabytes may seem like a lot, but remember that you're making room for program files, not just the information files you create.

▼ When talking hard disks, megabytes are cheaper by the dozen. The price you pay per megabyte plummets as the capacity of the hard disk increases.

▼ Both floppy disk drives and hard disk drives record information magnetically, much the way a tape recorder records music on a cassette tape. This process is called *saving*. Once you save your information on a disk, it stays there until you actively erase it. You can erase and rewrite information on the disks as many times as you want.

Monitors
(Up on the big screen)

It doesn't matter how fast and powerful your computer is if you can't see anything it does. That's why you need a monitor. The monitor shows you what you're typing, calculating, or what the computer is doing.

A computer monitor is more than just a screen. It also involves a circuit board that plugs into a slot inside the CPU, called the *video display adapter*. It's a little picture-making computer in itself. Your computer

tells the adapter what kinds of pictures to make, and the adapter builds them and sends them off to appear on your monitor screen. The fancier the picture you want, the more expensive the monitor, and the more expensive the video display adapter.

Monitors differ in the following three ways:

▼ size (13 to 15 inches is standard, bigger costs more)

▼ color capability (color monitors are more expensive than black-and-white monitors)

▼ number of colors (more colors makes the video display adapter more expensive)

Deciding how many colors are enough

▼ 16 colors—if you don't have a color printer and just want your programs to look nice on-screen

▼ 256 colors—if you have a color printer or want to create pages that will be commercially printed

▼ 64,000 colors—if you want to do serious graphic arts work, but don't have a big budget

▼ 16 million colors—if you're a graphic arts professional or are trying to keep up with the Joneses

PCs have several different display standards, which are different ways of creating images you see on screen. They're all known by acronyms (of course), and the one you want is VGA. It produces 16 colors and very crisp-looking text.

If you want more colors and even crisper looking text, you can opt for Super VGA. Super VGA actually covers a range of displays with progressively more colors and higher *resolution*—the number of tiny dots that the monitor uses to build its images.

At the Controls: Keyboards and Mice

The keyboard is the most common way to get letters, words, and numbers into the computer. If you've used a typewriter, you know how to use the keyboard.

An extension of the keyboard is a pointing device called a mouse. It attaches to the side of the keyboard. You roll it around, and a pointer (usually an arrow shape) on-screen moves correspondingly. You can use this pointer like a little finger to issue commands by pushing images of buttons that appear on-screen. You also can use the mouse to move things around on-screen or make drawings and artwork.

Options

Just as you can get air conditioning and a stereo in your new car, you can buy additional equipment, called *peripherals*, to complement your computer. A printer, for example, is a peripheral—probably the most useful one you can get. Peripheral vision is useful for spotting salesmen trying to sell you add-ons you don't want.

For the complete story on peripherals, consult Chapter 11. And remember: there are peripherals for every computer, so worry about the computer first, and sweat the peripherals later. (They don't call them peripheral for nothing.)

CHAPTER 3

Software
(Where the Real Work Gets Done)

IN A NUTSHELL

▼ What an operating system is

▼ What a program is

▼ Which comes first, the application or the computer?

▼ Major species of applications

▼ What exactly does a computer do with these programs, anyway?

I HATE BUYING A COMPUTER!

People talk about computers being hard—or easy—to use, but it's not the computer they're really talking about. It's the programs that run on the computer that are hard or easy, confusing or helpful. The computer is just a lump of circuits and chips.

But not all computers can run all programs. Just like you buy a different car for driving in town, on the open road, or tooling across the Gobi desert, you need a computer that matches your work.

This chapter has all you need to know about software but were hoping you wouldn't have to ask.

Arrrgh! There Are TWO Kinds of Software?!

Just when you thought it was safe to confidently bandy about the word *software*, it turns out there's more than one *kind* of software. The first kind of software is called the *operating system*. It takes care of all the low-level stuff, like showing things on the screen and filing stuff on the disk, so other programs can think about more important things. This is sort of like how part of your mind makes sure that your heart is beating, your lungs are breathing, and your eyes are blinking. It lets the rest of your mind concentrate on more important things, like what to watch on TV tonight. In the same way, with the operating system taking care of the basics, *application software* can do important tasks like word processing, spreadsheet making, and invading alien-zapping.

Operating System Software (The guy in the overalls)

The operating system (or "OS," if you're in the know) is one of those gotta-have-it parts of your computer. Because of that, it generally comes

with the computer. (If it isn't included, raise a fuss.) The operating system that comes built in with almost every PC is MS-DOS, version 5 or 6. Which should you get? Why, version 6, of course. When it comes to computer stuff, newer is almost always better.

DOS is not so friendly, which is why Que's book *I Hate DOS* has become a best-seller. (How's that for a shameless plug?) DOS is hard to understand and hard to work with. For that reason, many people have begun using *another* operating system with DOS—*Windows*. Windows is called "user friendly" because it presents program controls graphically (such as clearly labeled images of buttons to push) and "menus" of program instructions that are very easy to follow. The strange thing, though, is that you've got to have MS-DOS on your machine before you can use Windows; you can't use Windows without DOS.

So which should you use—DOS or Windows? Windows, definitely. It's much easier. The only drawback to Windows is that it requires more computing power.

Extra computer power requirements for running Windows

▼ A 386 computer: the faster the better

▼ At least an 80 megabyte hard drive

▼ At least 4 megabytes of memory

▼ A VGA monitor

▼ A mouse

CHAPTER 3

EXPERTS ONLY

An in-your-face explanation of interface

Interface. Ugly word! But, sadly, unavoidable. In computerese, an interface is where one thing (in this case, you) meets another (in this case, your application program).

To draw an everyday analogy, you could say that cars have a "standard user interface." When you buy a new car, you don't have to learn to drive all over again. You can count on the steering wheel working the same way in every car, with the same arrangements of pedals, more or less the same arrangement of dashboard gauges, and a rearview mirror in the expected position. It may take a week to find out how to work the high beams, but most things are predictable; you can learn the ins and outs of your new car quickly.

An operating system can function the same way, dictating to application programs how they will present themselves to you and how you will negotiate various tasks in the program. Windows and the Macintosh provide standard user interfaces that make them easy to use.

Application Programs (The specialists)

An application program—a word processor, for example—runs simultaneously and cooperatively (with any luck at all) with your computer's operating system. When the application needs some computer service done—getting data from a disk, for instance—it asks the operating system to do the work. In other words, you can think of the application program as running "on top of" the operating system, offering a set of higher functions, specific to your particular tasks. This is all done automatically, though, so you can try to forget it.

Sometimes, computer sellers toss in a free application program when you buy a computer—sometimes it may even be just the program you want to use. But typically you have to pay extra for application programs. Prices range from less than $100 to nearly $1,000 (that's right, as much as many computers).

BUZZWORDS

APPS

"Apps" is the hip way of saying "applications." In general, the computer crowd uses abbreviations as though saying whole words would cause their mouths to wear out prematurely.

Computers and Applications (Which is the chicken and which is the egg?)

Different software packages make different demands on a computer; some need a lot of power, for example, some a lot of memory. So do you decide on a program and then shop for a computer, or vice versa?

Most popular programs are designed to run on the most popular computers. You really don't have to tailor your computer to your application unless you're doing some pretty complicated stuff, such as working with big databases, engineering programs, or professional graphics and desktop publishing software.

When shopping, your best bet is to be able to accurately describe the "kind" of work you want to do. Informed computer salespeople can help you match the software you need with the computer that runs it well. You'll find specific tasks matched up to specific computer specs in Chapter 12.

I HATE BUYING A COMPUTER!

Major species of application programs

▼ *Word processors*. An electronic typist's assistant that records keystrokes, defines how a printed page will look, makes revisions easier, and performs high-speed miracles such as checking your spelling, alphabetizing things, and merging lists of addresses with stock letters to create your own junk mailings.

Minimum computer specs: 386, 2 megabytes of memory, 80 megabyte hard disk, black-and-white monitor

▼ *Spreadsheets*. An electronic balance sheet that revolutionized accounting by putting all those rows and columns of tiny numbers into the computer instead of on paper. Spreadsheet programs can do extraordinarily complex calculations based on the numbers in those rows and columns. Swindlers and embezzlers take note.

Minimum computer specs: 386, 2 megabytes of memory, 80 megabyte hard disk, black-and-white monitor

▼ *Graphics*. This group roughly subdivides into two subspecies: business graphics (such as charts and graphs) and graphic arts (illustration, drafting, photo retouching, and so on). Many of these programs can create slick results even if you don't have an artistic bone in your body.

Minimum computer specs: 386, 4 megabytes of memory, 120 megabyte hard disk, color monitor (at least 256 colors for professional purposes)

▼ *Databases*. These are filing programs for storing and retrieving information in myriad ways. They can be used for mailing lists, parts inventories, library catalogs, and keeping track of your enemies.

Minimum computer specs: 386, 4 megabytes of memory, 80 megabyte hard disk, black-and-white monitor

▼ *Desktop Publishing.* Basically, a way of making beautiful pages with whatever content you want: newsletters, books, magazines, posters, political creeds, and so forth. Available for aspiring Citizen Kanes with budgets large and small.

Minimum computer specs: 386, 4 megabytes of memory, 80 megabyte hard disk, color monitor (at least 256 colors for professional purposes)

▼ *Games.* You can fly a plane, fight off bad guys, or live out your fantasies (yes, *all* of them) with computer video games. These things should come with health warnings—they can be seriously habit forming.

Minimum computer specs: 386, 2 megabytes of memory, 80 megabyte hard disk, color monitor (the more colors, the more lifelike the display)

TIP

Application programs are often classified as "high end" or "low end" (or "entry level"). In general, high-end products are aimed at people who will be using them professionally, all day long.

Don't assume that low-end programs are incapable, amateurish, or beneath your dignity. Often they do just what you need (so you don't pay for capabilities you don't want or can't use), and their simplicity makes them easy to learn and use.

Putting It All Together
(Hardware + Software = What?)

When salespeople talk about computers, they like to talk about the process of computing. They expect you to somehow understand the mysterious flow of information in and out of the machine. So can I describe what a computer does in 25 words or less? You bet:

You give the computer some information and tell it what to do with it. When the job's done, it writes down the results for later use. Simple.

Here are some examples:

▼ Type in some text in a word-processing program, tell the computer to make it look like a business letter, tell the computer to print it, and then file away the electronic version of the letter.

▼ Type in some numbers in a spreadsheet program, tell the computer to create an annual budget, and then save the spreadsheet it creates for use later.

▼ Feed the computer a list of addresses from another computer, tell your computer to sort them by ZIP code and print each one on an envelope, and save the sorted mailing list for later.

All of a computer's chores follow this same basic pattern: load data in, fiddle with it, and send it back out. Or, in computerese, input, processing, and output.

BUZZWORDS

DATA

This term has the same meaning as "information," but sounds more high-tech. It's also easier to type for people like me, who use two fingers.

Remember this!

▼ A computer can't do anything without software—sets of instructions that adapt the computer for specific jobs, such as typing, making pictures, or doing math calculations.

▼ A computer uses two kinds of programs: operating system software to manage the mechanics of the computer, and application programs that *you* use to manage and transform information.

▼ Application programs perform specific jobs and meet specific needs, whether it's creating a business letter, an architect's rendering, or a financial table.

CHAPTER 4

PC or Mac?
(That Is the Question)

IN A NUTSHELL

▼ Why only PC or Mac?

▼ Compatibility and clones

▼ Dueling hardware: Mac vs. PC

▼ Operating systems: DOS, the Mac System, and Windows

▼ So which one is better?

I HATE BUYING A COMPUTER!

Let's trim your purchasing decision down to size. The personal computer market is divided into three parts: PC compatibles, Apple Macintoshes, and the also-rans. This third and sorry lot includes such capable computers as the Commodore Amiga and the Atari. By cruel fate, corporate malfeasance, or astrological mischance, these machines have been left in the dust.

So this chapter helps you tackle your most basic buying decision: Do you want a PC, or do you want a Mac? What's the difference between the two?

Wait a Minute! Why Only a PC or a Mac?

No philosophical discussion here—the issues are strictly practical. PCs and Macs are the best choices because they offer the following:

▼ The widest selection of application programs

▼ Greater resale value

▼ Compatibility with millions of other computers

▼ Easy access to free advice from other owners

The smart money says to be a conformist and buy a Mac or PC.

TIP

Macintoshes and PCs aren't as different as they used to be. In their competition for the bigger slice of the market pie, Macs and PCs—like Republicans and Democrats—have tended to become more like each other.

CAUTION

Pay little heed to anyone who gushes passionately about the joys of working with one brand of computer or another—such a person is a dangerous nut who has lost perspective on what's important in life.

On the other hand, listen closely to people who rave and rant and vent their hatred of their computers. These people you can learn things from.

Compatibility and Clones
(Is owning a clone like having a fake Gucci?)

There are dozens of companies that make IBM PC-compatible computers—the so-called clones. What makes these clones compatible is a very similar hardware setup—including the same kind of microprocessor. And they all run the same operating system. Clones are good (unless you're IBM); they save you a lot of money. And many companies build their PCs every bit as well as IBM. There's no shame in owning a non-IBM PC.

On the other hand, there is no such thing as a Macintosh compatible. Anyone who tries to sell you one will probably make you a deal on the Brooklyn Bridge as well. Apple protects the Macintosh design with a formidable array of patents and attack-lawyers.

BUZZWORDS

CLONE

A clone is a piece of hardware or software that copies the performance of another so closely that its behavior is (ideally) indistinguishable from the original. Imitation may be the sincerest form of flattery, but in this case, it's also a common source of lawsuits for copyright and patent infringement.

Battle Lines: The PC-Mac Match-Up

So what's the difference between the Macintosh and the PC? Not much, from a hardware point of view. One machine doesn't do things particularly better than the other—just differently.

Each machine has its strong suits and its weak ones. In the end, your best strategy is to sit in front of both of them, see which you prefer, consult your checkbook, and buy the one you prefer.

Price

For computers of equivalent power and capability, PCs are considerably cheaper than Macs. Why? Good old-fashioned competition. Lots of companies are making PCs, but only one makes Macintoshes.

Without a doubt, you get more bang for your buck from a PC.

Advantage: PC

Standards (Put tab A into slot B—if you can find it)

In the PC world, there are many hardware standards—industry-accepted ways of making various pieces of the computer work together. This means that when combining diverse parts to build a single PC system, all the parts have to be adjusted to work with each other. Then your programs have to be adjusted to the computer. This can be a pain in the neck, and it's a process best left to the people you buy your computer from.

In the much narrower Macintosh universe, almost all standards are defined by Apple, so hardware incompatibilities are almost unknown. Programs adjust to the hardware automatically. Very little fiddling is needed to get all the pieces humming in harmony.

Advantage: Macintosh

Physical Differences (No PC-to-Mac organ transplants)

Because PC and Mac microprocessors are different, programs written for each one have to be created differently, written in the "language of the chip." You can't use a Mac program on a PC, or vice versa (although many programs have a version for each machine).

The parts of Macs and PCs aren't interchangeable either, just as Ford and Chevy parts can't be swapped. But like Ford and Chevy, the machines are functionally much more alike than they are different.

Advantage: Dead heat

Writing Style (Different . . . but not too)

Macs and PCs can use the same disks, but each records information to the disks differently; one machine can't necessarily read the disks of another. And the information created by each computer is itself written in different ways (in a different language, as it were); hence, a PC can't always read a Macintosh file, and vice versa.

With the proper software, however, you can easily connect Macs and PCs together to share information. At one time, it was difficult to get the two machines to talk to each other, but that's no longer the case. So-called file translation software is cheap and easy to use.

So if you have a Mac but need to swap files with an associate who has a PC, you don't have to go out and buy a PC. A PC can trade files with a Mac perfectly well. Likewise, PC owners can integrate a Mac into their office with ease.

Advantage: Even-steven

Application Programs (A win/win situation)

Neither Mac nor PC has an advantage in the quality, range, or price of the software available. In fact, most top-notch programs have versions for both PCs and Macs, and these versions are generally functionally identical (and usually cost the same, too). Your choices include word processors, spreadsheets, desktop publishing programs, and graphics programs.

Advantage: You

Macs and PCs: A View from the Operating System

If you've already read Chapter 3, you know that a computer's operating system largely defines the "look and feel" of the program on any computer. This isn't just a decorative issue: you will be more productive on the machine that you're more comfortable using. (Life's too short to waste time cursing your computer.)

On the Macintosh, you have no choice of operating systems. There's only one, and most Mac users don't even think of it as a separate program—it's simply the personality of the machine.

On the PC, you have two options: the older, cheaper, harder-to-use DOS, and the newer Microsoft Windows, a cheery graphical cover-up for DOS that gives the PC a user-friendly persona like the Mac. Windows makes PC computing pleasant; if you buy a PC, you'll probably want Windows.

The Macintosh System

The Macintosh simplified computing by creating a rigid set of standards for how programs should behave. These rules are prescribed by the *System*, the ominous name of the Mac operating system. All commands and program functions are written in plain English. They're logically laid out in menus and control panels. If you know how to use one Mac program, learning others is easy.

DOS

Today's basic PC operating system—DOS—has evolved from the original PC operating system, designed way back in the dark ages of the early '80s. Under the operating rules laid down by DOS, no two application programs need to look alike or work alike. Opening a program for the first time is like entering a new and unfamiliar world. Some people like chaos.

DOS has been upgraded many times, but it still represents old-style, science-fair computing. If you want to get something done—like starting a program or looking at a listing of files on a disk—you have to type in a command, often expressed in obtuse computer codes. You have to remember commands such as:

DIR C:/p

CHKDSK

FORMAT B: /f:720

COPY A:*.* B:

Sounds like fun, doesn't it? DOS is so awkward to use that it's the focus of more computer how-to books than any other subject.

BUZZWORDS

DOS

DOS (rhymes with "floss") stands for "disk operating system." It operates more than disks these days, but back in the murky past when DOS was first cooked up, operating a disk was considered a big deal.

Microsoft Windows

Windows is Microsoft's latest attempt to uplift DOS, and it has been very successful. Windows takes the Macintosh approach of a standard user interface and applies it to the chaotic world of PCs, with its dozens of standards for how hardware and software should perform.

The result is something that was unthinkable even a few years ago: an easy-to-use PC. The interface is graphical and intuitive; children can figure it out. Adults too.

BUZZWORDS

INTUITIVE

These days, calling software "intuitive" is the highest praise you can give to a program. Translated into plain English, this means "It's so easy to use, you don't even have to read the manual." But if programs were so darned intuitive, there wouldn't be so many how-to computer books on the market, would there?

Windows' principal problem is that buried inside it (but not quite deep enough) lurks DOS. So even though you spend most of your time working with an easy-to-use interface, you still have to deal with DOS and its obscure command language from time to time.

Reasons to stick with DOS

▼ There's a price to pay for the deluxe services Windows offers, just as you have to pay extra to stay in a four-star hotel. If all you need is a roof over your head and a bug-free bed, you can stick with DOS, the equivalent of Uncle Bob's Koze-E-Kabins. One of the charms of Uncle Bob's, er, DOS, is that it's cheaper than Windows.

continues

▼ Windows requires a powerful (and more expensive) computer. The latest version of Windows calls for a near-top-of-the-line PC.

▼ Some applications—and some users—don't need a friendly, pretty interface. They just need a straightforward application program, and many major PC programs run faster and better in their DOS versions than their Windows versions.

And the Winner Is?

After it's set up and running your programs, the Mac has no advantage over the PC, or vice versa. You might prefer some of the particulars of how one or the other operates, but that's really just a matter of what you get used to. Maybe the fact that the PC limits you to 8-character-long file names is enough to drive you to use a Mac, which can use 32-character file names. But probably not.

When something in your computer system changes, however, the Mac has the upper hand. Add a new piece of hardware to a PC, such as a monitor, printer, or modem, and you've got some serious tinkering and manual-reading on your hands. Making changes on the PC can create a ripple effect that takes some time and effort to calm down. Such configuration problems on the Macintosh are rare.

The PC's main advantage is popularity. With a PC, you'll have less trouble finding someone who can help you with problems. When it comes time to share files with other computers, your chances of having compatible files is better if you're using a PC. Further, many Macintoshes can read PC disks now—so you're covered either way with PC files.

The bulk of this book assumes that, like most people, you'll be getting a PC compatible. Don't worry, though—there are plenty of good tips for you if you decide on a Mac. Both types of computers are winners.

Remember this!

▼ The two most popular personal computers (and the only logical choices for your purchase) are PC compatibles (made by several dozen manufacturers) and Macintoshes (made exclusively by Apple Computer).

▼ The term *PC* refers to personal computers modeled after the original IBM PC design. They're called *PC compatibles* because they all use very similar hardware and, more importantly, can all run the same programs.

▼ From your point of view as you sit at the keyboard, there's no big difference between PC hardware and Macintosh hardware. The two computers cannot exchange parts, but the parts of both types work basically the same way.

▼ The principal difference between the Mac and PC is the operating systems they use.

▼ The PC uses two operating systems. The first, DOS, manages the basic functions of the computer. The second, Microsoft Windows, is built on top of DOS to create an easy-to-use graphic interface. Many PC applications need Windows to operate—many need only DOS.

▼ The Mac has one operating system, which always comes with the computer.

CHAPTER 5
Bundles of Joy

IN A NUTSHELL

▼ What's a bundle, and what's in one?
▼ Basic PC bundles
▼ Basic Macintosh bundles
▼ Preconfiguration

I HATE BUYING A COMPUTER!

I f you've spent time looking at computer magazines, you've probably seen roundups of the 50 best monitor bargains, the top 100 hard disks on the market, and the 200 most popular mice. "What the)?!&(*% is this?" you probably shrieked. "Doesn't all this stuff just *come* with the computer?" Well, yes and no. You *can* buy each piece separately—which can be about as much fun as fending off a pit bull—or you can buy all the components for the system in one super, handy-dandy package (called a *bundle*).

In this chapter, you learn about how computers are sold, and how to save your sanity by buying a complete computer system instead of individual components.

The System Is the Solution

The best computer deals come as *bundles*, which is a cuddly way of saying that you write one check for a stack of boxes containing pieces that are guaranteed to work together. If you ask, "Can I get that with a TurboZip 500 BitWhiz Hard Drive as gushed about in *PC World* magazine?" the answer will almost surely be "No." Instead, you'll be told that the hard disk in the machine you're buying will do just fine, which is probably the truth—or pretty darn close.

When you shop for a computer, then, you're looking for the best price on the bundle of your choice. Fortunately, enough variations are available out there that you can find a bundle to match your needs and your pocketbook.

BUZZWORDS

SYSTEM

The all-purpose word *system* is used generically to describe a complete computer setup: CPU, keyboard, monitor, operating system software, and perhaps a mouse and printer.

CAUTION

Many computer ads contain a tiny line of type hiding in some corner: *Monitor not included.* This little line allows advertisers to legitimately create an eye-catching price that can be displayed prominently, in great big type. Beware. This is the computer ad equivalent of a car being sold at a great price—steering wheel and clutch extra. Sneaky indeed. Whenever you buy a computer system, make sure that you're getting all the parts you expect.

PC Bundles

Because the design of the PC is basically community property, over the years everybody in the community has devised his or her own way to make it run. The result is that if you buy a CPU here, a hard drive there, and a keyboard somewhere else, there is no guarantee that all the pieces will actually work together. To make the pieces compatible, somebody has got to fiddle with the wiring and read through all the manuals and utter a couple magic chants. And believe me, you don't want to be the one to do it.

The PC bundle you buy should be *preconfigured*, a term that sounds suspiciously religious. But it basically means that someone has already adjusted the pieces to work together, and can guarantee you that the whole

thing functions as it should. Blessed are the bundle-makers, for they shall bring harmony to the desktop.

Is That PC Loaded?

If you decide to buy a PC, insist that it come with the operating system already installed on the hard disk. If you're planning to use Microsoft Windows, insist that it be installed on the hard disk as well. Granted, installing DOS and Windows is not necessarily an onerous task for you to do, but it has the potential to get you off on the wrong foot with your computer. Your first day of computing should be one of quizzical wonder, not stupefaction and bewilderment.

You can also buy a PC with the operating system *and* some applications already on the hard disk. In this case, setting up your computer could not be easier. You connect the monitor and keyboard to the CPU, plug it in, turn it on, and stare in wonder at your already-functionable computer. Within seconds you can start publishing your own newspaper, challenging Wall Street, or training your lasers on invading space ships.

Checklist

✔ You get the best price on a computer when you buy all the parts in a bundle. As when buying a complete stereo system, you don't get as many component choices, but you get a much lower price and a lot less hassle.

✔ Look for a computer that has software included.

✔ Buy your computer *preconfigured*—all set up and ready to run with no fiddling or adjusting on your part.

Basic Macintosh Bundles

Macintosh systems have always been bundled, because you could never buy Mac parts from anyone but Apple and its dealers. The exception is monitors and printers, which Apple has deigned to allow others to manufacture for use with Macs. Still, you can get a matched CPU, keyboard, mouse, and custom monitor (a non-Apple one, that is) from almost any Apple dealer.

Operating system software is always included with Macintosh bundles. Typically, you have to install this yourself, but it isn't a complicated process. Macintosh manuals assume that you have a single-digit I.Q.

TIP

Many Macintosh dealers offer systems that include a monitor from some company other than Apple. If you decide to buy one, have the dealer install it for you (it requires lifting the lid of the computer and installing a special circuit board). If you've never used a computer before—or even if you have—you probably don't want to be taking the lid off the thing on the first day and sticking your hands inside among all those fragile little parts and wires.

CHAPTER 6
The Test Drive

IN A NUTSHELL

▼ What to look for
▼ The ins and outs of graphical interfaces
▼ Basic computer maneuvers
▼ Taking the controls
▼ The 10 commandments
   of computer demos

CHAPTER 6

Taking a computer for a test spin before you buy it is important. But what do you test? You don't want to just start punching keys because you won't learn anything that way, and you may look silly to the computer salesperson. This chapter prepares you to slip comfortably behind the driver's wheel, er, keyboard, and see whether the machine's up to snuff.

First, you'll take a look at what you can expect to see on the screen, and then you'll take a look at the kinds of driving tests you want to do in the showroom.

What You'll Probably See On-Screen

Think about whenever you've made a big purchase, like a car or a house. Did the salesperson just point you toward the most average-looking, run-of-the-mill aspects? No way. He showed you the gee-whiz stuff. Well, the same thing happens with computers. Salespeople will undoubtedly show you a color computer running a really snappy graphics program.

Those programs are fine, but remember that once you *buy* the computer, you probably won't run that flight simulator demo—you'll use it to do real work. Have the salesperson run a program similar to the kind of programs you will use on your computer. If you're going to be writing, have him run a word-processing program. If you're going to be managing your finances, have him start a spreadsheet or personal finance package.

This Is DOS?

Using DOS and DOS programs can be complicated. DOS doesn't define what programs should look like or how they work, so no two DOS programs look alike. And DOS itself is more than a little abstract.

If you're test driving a computer that uses DOS, you'll probably start out at a blank screen with something called a *prompt*. A prompt is DOS's way of asking for instructions. At the DOS prompt, you can type in DOS commands (format a disk, list the contents of a disk, and so forth), or you can type in the name of a program. Hit the Return or Enter key (a leftover from the bygone typewriter days) and DOS carries out your command.

Things you can type at a DOS prompt during a test drive

▼ Type **DIR** and press Enter to see a list of the files in the current directory. Don't bother looking at the list that appears; it doesn't mean anything. What matters is how fast the list zips by. If files go by so fast you don't have a clue as to what they say, the computer is fast enough.

▼ Type **prompt (your name here) is the coolest$g** and press Enter. Ha ha! You have now replaced that ugly C:\> with your own personal assertion of hipness! Congratulations, you've just entered the wonderful world of computer pranks.

▼ Type **EDIT** and press Enter to go to a text editor that comes with DOS. You can practice typing and erasing in this program to see whether you like the feel of the keyboard. An important thing to check is whether you're comfortable with the Tab, Backspace, and Delete keys because you'll want easy access to those in most programs.

If the Demo Does Windows...

PCs using Microsoft Windows are much easier to test drive than computers running DOS. Instead of having to type commands in some forgotten dialect of Sanskrit, you move a mouse pointer to what you want

to do and double-click. After you mess around with one or two Windows programs, you'll know enough to be dangerous in just about any Windows program.

Reasons that graphical interfaces are all the rage

▼ They make it easier for developers to write creative, useful programs. (Does this mean that application programs will become cheaper? Dream on.)

▼ They make programs easier to learn. You can usually figure out the major functions of a program without ever reading the instruction manual.

▼ You don't have to remember how to get things done in a program because most of it is self-explanatory. You can use a program profitably even if you don't use it often enough to memorize all its functions.

▼ You usually see on-screen an accurate preview of how your printed page will look.

Mousing Around

Both Mac and Windows use a mouse to get things done, as a mouse works well in graphical programs. Example: You don't have to type the command Print to print a page. Instead, you use the mouse to point at an image of a button labeled Print, or better yet, a picture of a printer. Pushing the button on the mouse (also known as *clicking*) pushes the button on-screen, and the command is carried out. This feature is great for people like me who type with two fingers and can't type **print** without having to make several corrections. It also means you don't have to learn a bunch of code words to operate the program. Just look at the menus and buttons and click in the right places.

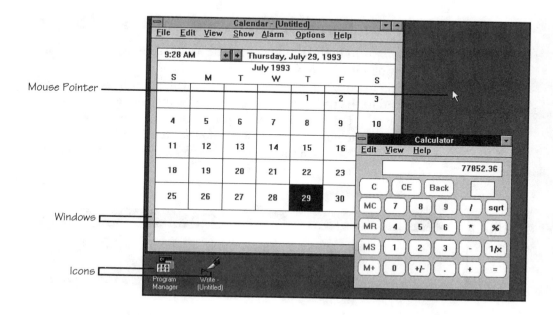

Mouse Pointer —

Windows

Icons

▼ The appearance of the mouse pointer changes according to where it is on-screen. When its shape changes, its capabilities change too. As an arrow, for example, you can use it to give orders to the program.

▼ One click of the mouse button selects something. When something is selected, you can do things to it (move it, copy it, change its color, delete it, etc).

▼ Holding down the mouse button while you slide the mouse (a maneuver called *dragging*) is another common technique. You use it to select text, for example, before you change its appearance or copy it to a new location.

▼ With a two-button mouse, the left-hand button does almost all of the work.

I HATE BUYING A COMPUTER!

One Picture Is Worth a Thousand Software Manuals

The emphasis in both Windows and the Mac system is on graphically representing information whenever possible. For example, programs and files are represented graphically by symbols (like that little printer image mentioned in the preceding section) called *icons*. Move the mouse pointer until it points to an icon of your word processing program, quickly click the mouse button twice (*double-click*), and the program starts up. Double-click a file icon, and the program that created it starts up and opens the file you selected.

BUZZWORDS

WINDOW

A window is a rectangular screen within a screen in which programs run and your work appears. You can have several windows open at once. It's like having several pieces of paper on your desk at the same time.

You can position one window on top of another (just like paper documents), or you can position them side-by-side to compare documents. You can change the width and height of these windows so that you can see things that are lurking behind them, such as other windows. You resize or move windows by using the mouse.

What's on the Menu?

The last major feature of graphical environments are lists of program options called menus, whose titles are shown in a band along the top of the screen. When you move the mouse pointer to point at one of these

titles, a menu drops down from it, listing possible commands you can issue or actions you can take. For instance, a menu entitled File might list options to Open a File, Make a New File, Close a File, Save a File, Save a File With a New Name, Print a File, and so forth.

On the Mac, you drag down a menu to make a selection from it. When you've dragged down to the option you want, release the mouse button and your command is carried out. In Windows, click a menu to make it drop down. To select an option, move the pointer to that option and click once.

When a program has menus, you don't have to memorize any program commands. They're all there, listed clearly and organized logically.

Fearlessly Taking Over the Controls

If you've never sat at a computer before, your first thought will likely be, "Oh no. I'm going to destroy something. I'm going to erase everything, sizzle the chips, and make smoke billow out of the disk drives." Don't worry—you can't do any damage. Just grab the mouse, aim the pointer at something, click the mouse button once or twice, and see what happens.

Computer programs these days are smart; if you do something potentially destructive, a warning message pops up on-screen, such as `Pushing that button will start World War III. Are you sure you want to continue?` When in doubt, click the Cancel button. And remember, there's no shame in asking the salesperson for help in using a program. Even certified techno-dweebs have to ask for help in operating computers that aren't theirs.

TIP

When you're getting demonstrations of computers, make clear to the salespeople that you want to compare computers, not application programs. A good strategy is to see the same program—one that you'd likely use yourself—on a range of different machines. That way, you'll be comparing the performance of the machines, not the relative glitter and gloss of the programs that run on it.

Demonstrations Are Nice, but Do-It-Yourself Is Better

Computer salespeople like to show off. They'll have the screen dancing, type flying, illustrations spinning, and your mind boggling. Their hands will be a blur, flashing from keyboard to mouse and back. All this activity is interesting, but not always instructive. It's better for you to sit at the controls and experience the machine yourself. It's the only way to get a good feel for your prospective purchase.

TIP

When you're testing a computer, test it running software you're likely to use. Graphics are cool, but if you're going to be doing word processing, who cares about putting a mustache on the Mona Lisa?

The 10 commandments of computer demos

▼ Ask lots of questions—no question is dumb if you don't know the answer.

▼ Take the controls yourself and have the salesperson walk you though some typical tasks that you'd be doing in your day-to-day work. Don't be rushed!

▼ If something happened too fast for you to see or understand, ask the salesperson to do it again.

▼ If you're trying to look cool, don't pick up the mouse and look underneath it (there's just a little ball down there, anyway).

▼ Get a good feel for the keyboard and the mouse; they vary from machine to machine.

▼ Check out a couple of competing programs on the same computer to see what the programs are doing, as opposed to the computer.

▼ Don't move any computer components except the keyboard and mouse. Lifting the monitor will give you instant back problems.

▼ Ask for plain-English explanations of things you don't understand, and remember the magic words: "Why is that important?"

▼ Have the salesperson go away for a little while so you can play around unobserved. With less pressure, you'll begin to notice important things about what you like and dislike about the computer.

▼ Take notes about each computer you see: good monitor/bad monitor, crisp keyboard/mushy keyboard, fast/slow, and so forth. It's the only way to remember the differences among similar machines.

PART II

The Major Variables and What They Cost

Includes:

CHAPTER 7

Speed and Power
(It's in the Chips)

IN A NUTSHELL

- ▼ What makes a computer powerful
- ▼ What makes one computer faster than another
- ▼ What makes one fast computer even faster than another
- ▼ The price of power
- ▼ Software for faster computing

P ower is good, and more power is better. Oh sure, now you think I sound like a greedy corporate-raider type, but I'm talking about *computer* power here. What makes a computer powerful? And how does computer power translate into practical terms? Read this chapter to find out.

Brain Power

For the most part, the power of a computer is defined by what its microprocessor can do. Like the circus strongman at the base of a human pyramid, the broader its shoulders, the more performers it can support.

And what makes one microprocessor more powerful than another? Basically, two things: how fast it works and how much information it can process at one time.

If all this power talk makes you nervous, think about speed instead. The more powerful the computer, the faster it runs, and when you're working with a computer, faster is always better. If you want to be able to get serious work done on your computer, you should get either an 80386-based machine (commonly called 386s) or, if you want to be state of the art and you have a little extra to spend, get an 80486 (called 486s, for short). Anything else will leave you bored and frustrated by its slowness.

Shopping by Numbers

In order to create maximum confusion for consumers, microprocessor chips are known by number. Luckily, there aren't many of these numbers, and they're logically numbered—bigger is better. And, not surprisingly, more powerful chips mean more expensive computers.

The following tables list the processors available today.

PC microprocessors

Processor	Pronounced	Comments
8088	eighty eighty-eight	The original PC chip
8086	eighty eighty-six	The first PC chip to support hard disks
80286	two eighty-six	The chip in AT-class PCs
80386SX	three eighty-six S X	The minimum to run Windows
80386	three eighty-six	Currently the most popular processor
80486SX	four eighty-six S X	Just slightly better than an 80386
80486	four eighty-six	Top-of-the-line in power and speed
Pentium	Pentium	Beyond powerful, beyond fast, beyond expensive

Mac microprocessors

Processor	Pronounced	Comments
68000	sixty-eight thousand	The original Mac chip, now obsolete

continues

I HATE BUYING A COMPUTER!

Processor	Pronounced	Comments
68020	sixty-eight-oh-twenty	The minimum for today's programs
68030	sixty-eight-oh-thirty	Faster, better, more expensive
68040	sixty-eight-oh-forty	Top-of-the-line in power and speed

Remember that in both Mac and PC processor families, the higher the number of the chip, the more powerful the chip is. At any given time, the chips in the top-of-the-line Macs and PCs are more or less equal in what they can do.

TIP

For most business purposes, PC compatibles based on 8088, 8086, and 80286 chips are now considered obsolete—the latest software has outgrown them. You should be able to buy a used one for a song, or even the threat of a song. For information about buying used equipment, see Chapter 16.

"I HATE THIS!"

SX, DX, #$*@!!!

PC microprocessors sometimes have letters appended to their numerical names, making them sound more like a BMW model than a computer part. The suffix SX (as in 386SX) indicates that the processor isn't quite as powerful as the regular version of the chips. To keep the regular old chips from falling into a blue funk, they've been given the fancy suffix DX,

which simply means "not an SX." In short, DX chips are faster; SX chips are slower.

Computer Speeds

The speed of a computer is regulated by an internal timer like the quartz crystal used in most battery-powered clocks. But the ticking of a computer's internal clock—its *clock speed*—is incredibly fast. It's a metronome for music played at the speed of light. Computer salespeople like to talk about clock speed because it's the computer equivalent of horsepower. The faster the clock ticks; the faster the computer is.

BUZZWORDS

CLOCK SPEED

Computer clock speeds are rated in megahertz (MHz). One megahertz equals one million clock ticks per second. Today's faster personal computers operate at clock speeds in excess of 50 MHz—50 million ticks per second. This speed enables computer operators to make errors faster than ever before.

The clock speed of the computer usually comes right after the type of processor you're using. For example, if you're looking at an 80386 with a clock speed of 25, the computer salesperson calls it a 386-25. If you're looking at the latest and fastest—an 80486 with a clock speed of 66, you can say, offhandedly, "Say, a 486-66. Not bad. Can you accept my house as a down payment on this computer?"

Why does clock speed matter? It matters because everything in the computer has to be synchronized to the pace set by its internal clock. The faster the clock speed, the faster your programs can run.

How fast is fast enough?

▼ A 386SX-16 is the slowest machine you should consider. It can run Windows, but just barely.

▼ The 386-25 was the mid-range business computer of choice until fairly recently. Computer geeks are beginning to turn their noses up at these machines now.

▼ 486-33s are plenty fast for most applications now.

▼ 486-50s will easily take care of all your computer needs for at least a couple of years. If you get one of these, your computer friends will begin to hang around your computer, asking if they can use it "just for a minute."

▼ A 486-66 is overkill for most people. For people who work with giant graphics or desktop publishing, however, it's a dream come true.

EXPERTS ONLY

A lot faster isn't always a lot better

Although higher clock speeds mean faster computing, the relationship between clock speed and operating speed is not clear-cut. A computer running at 50 MHz is not necessarily anywhere near twice as fast as one running at 25 MHz. The reason for this discrepancy is that operating speed depends on the software you're using, the kinds of tasks the program is performing, and the speed at which other parts of the computer, such as the disk drives, are operating. The computer with the faster clock speed will indeed run faster, but how much faster is hard to say.

Likewise, comparing the clock speeds of Macintoshes and PCs doesn't tell you anything because these machines' microprocessors and software are so different.

"I HATE THIS!"

My computer isn't fast enough!

There's no such thing as a fast-enough computer. The machine whose speed has you saying "gee whiz" today will have you growling in six months, drumming your fingers on the table, and muttering, "Hurry up, you lumbering sow." Or words to that effect.

Processing Power: The Computer as Information Pump

This section explains the other reason why some computers run faster than others. Information pipes run to and from the microprocessor, and the wider these pipes are, the faster information can move, and the faster the computer runs. The microprocessor also has internal plumbing, and wider pipes make for faster processing.

The width of these pipes is measured in bits. You want your microprocessor to have the biggest pipes—called *data paths*—available: 32-bits wide for both internal and external plumbing. Watch out for microprocessors that have 32-bit internal piping but only 16-bit pipes leading in and out. You don't want your pipes backing up, do you?

TIP

When you're shopping for a computer, especially when you're shopping for a PC, you'll hear confusing claims about 16- and 32-bit processing. Now that you know what it means—and how simple it is—when you're confronted with frothy marketing hype, you can just look bored.

EXPERTS ONLY

Bits and bytes

The basic units of computer information are *bits* and *bytes*, terms that computer aficionados can use with a completely straight face. To communicate, humans make words out of letters. A computer makes words out of 1's and 0's—that's its entire alphabet.

A *bit* is the smallest thing a computer can say or understand: a choice between 1 and 0, yes and no. Not much of a vocabulary.

A *byte* is a string of eight bits taken together to form an 8-letter "word." Using those eight 1's an 0's, a byte has 256 possible spellings, hence 256 possible meanings. All the bits inside a computer are organized into bytes, so the byte is a handy unit for measuring information volume, such as the size of a file or the capacity of a computer's memory.

Special Speed Chips

Special accelerator chips called *coprocessors* can speed up a computer by lending a helping hand when the microprocessor is doing particularly

arduous tasks. There are two popular types of coprocessors, both of which are common options in both Macs and PCs.

▼ *Math coprocessors* handle specific math functions and execute them at very high speed. Not all programs can take advantage of a math coprocessor, but those that do include graphics, technical, and mathematical packages, such as spreadsheets.

▼ A *graphics coprocessor* handles elaborate graphics (there's some logic to this stuff), especially complex photographic and video images.

TIP

Before investing in a coprocessor (they cost extra), make sure the application programs you intend to use can actually take advantage of them. This fact is usually written right on the box the program comes in.

EXPERTS ONLY

Cold hard cache

There are several software tricks for speeding up a computer. The one used (and advertised) most often is called *caching*. Caching means that if the computer thinks you're going to need certain information more than once, it keeps that information close by, where the computer can get to it more quickly the next time you need it. The answer to a complex calculation, for example, can be *cached* to save the computer from having to perform the same calculation again later.

Similarly, instructions written in certain chips inside the computer can be copied into a memory *cache*, where the processor can get at them faster. Some hard disks also use memory caches to speed up the traffic of information to and from the disk.

High-Speed Software

A more powerful microprocessor can also contribute to improved performance by giving new capabilities to the software programs it supports. The most dramatic of these contributions is the ability to perform *multitasking*, which is the ability for the computer to do two or more tasks at the same time.

The newer generation of microprocessors are so powerful that, in effect, they can divide themselves into several parts, with each part independently carrying out its own task. In practical terms, this capability means that you write business letters at the same time that your computer is doing a 10-minute search through a large database. You don't have to wait for the computer to finish one task before you embark on another. Multitasking can make you so productive that you may self-combust—take care!

On a PC, you need Windows and an 80386 or (better yet) 80486 chip to run multitasking programs; on a Mac, you need a 68030 or 68040 chip.

Remember this!

▼ The microprocessor (chip) is the brain of your computer. These chips are known by number, and succeeding generations of personal computers use increasingly powerful microprocessors.

▼ The speed of a microprocessor is called its clock speed. The clock speed measures how fast the chip can carry out program instructions.

▼ The processing power of a chip is measured by how many bits of information it can process simultaneously.

▼ Special speed chips called coprocessors can make a computer run faster.

▼ Multitasking software lets you do more things with your computer at once.

CHAPTER 8

Memory and Disk Storage

(Save Me!)

IN A NUTSHELL

- ▼ Hard disks vs. floppy disks
- ▼ Kinds and sizes of disks
- ▼ Capacities of diskettes
- ▼ PC diskettes vs. Mac diskettes
- ▼ Hard disk capacities
- ▼ Hard disk prices
- ▼ Memory—why your computer needs it
- ▼ How much memory is enough?
- ▼ Expanding your computer's memory in the future

There are two ways to store information on a computer: temporarily (in memory) and permanently (on disks). And today's computers have big appetites for both kinds of storage.

Memory is a computer's work space—the blackboard where it does its calculating. The computer uses it, erases it, and uses it again thousands of times in the course of a working day. *Disks* are where a computer writes down the results of its work; they're the permanent archive.

When you buy a computer, you'll have to decide how much memory you need and how much disk storage you need. It's not a tough decision, and the next few pages contain everything you need to know to make a wise choice.

A Tale of Two Disks

To be stored permanently—or *saved* (a surprisingly straightforward term)—computer information is recorded onto *disks*. Computer disks store information magnetically, just the way music is recorded on a cassette tape. And like a cassette tape, you can erase and re-record a disk over and over again.

You put disks into something called a *disk drive*, which is like a little Walkman that can record as well as play back—or access—information. The disk drive has a magnetic record/playback head like a tape recorder that swings across the surface of the disk, storing information or reading back things that are already there.

There are two common types of storage disks:

▼ Diskettes, which are portable, like compact discs, and hold a modest amount of information.

▼ Hard disks, which are permanently mounted in their disk drives and hold enormous amounts of information.

HUH?

BUZZWORDS

ACCESS

Access is a $2 way of saying "get at." For example, a computer *accesses* the information on a disk. Hard disk drives are rated according to how long it takes them to get at information on the disk, a statistic called *access time*. I suppose that this is more elegant than saying get-at-it time.

Diskettes (a.k.a. floppy disks, a.k.a. floppies)

Diskettes—also called *floppy disks*—are removable and fit into a slot in the front of the computer. They make your information portable; you can carry a diskette around in your pocket. When you want to feed new information or programs into your computer, you can do it via diskettes. You'll definitely need at least one floppy disk drive for your computer, but it's better to get two—one of each size.

A diskette consists of a thin, flexible—yes, floppy—plastic disk that's held in a plastic housing. This housing protects the surface of the disk from dust and crud. A diskette can be wrecked by getting it wet, smudging it with fingerprints, or getting cracker crumbs inside it.

Diskettes come in different sizes and capacities (much like cassette tapes) and hold the equivalent of several hundred pages of simple text. Through the miracle of modern programming, though, some programs (especially desktop publishing programs) can now create pages that are so complicated—filled with illustrations, color, and photographs—that you can't even fit one of them on a diskette. That's progress.

"I HATE THIS!"

Alas, my diskette is dead!

Diskettes die. Suddenly and without warning. No, it's not a very friendly thing for a technology that calls itself "permanent storage." It's like having your boat permanently stored at the bottom of the lake. To avert such tragedies, all diskettes should be backed up—in other words, you should have two electronic copies of everything. Sensible paranoids put the two versions in different places; having two copies doesn't do you any good if you can drown them both in the same Pepsi spill.

Checklist

✔ There are two sizes of floppy disks: 5 1/4-inch and 3 1/2-inch. Older PCs use only the 5 1/4-inch ones, whereas newer models can use either. Macintoshes use only 3 1/2-inch diskettes.

✔ Although bigger, 5 1/4-inch diskettes don't hold more information than 3 1/2-inch diskettes. And whereas 3 1/2-inch diskettes are protected by a nice rigid plastic case, 5 1/4-inch diskettes take the name "floppy" a little too seriously. Their thin plastic housing is far from rigid, and with one false move, you can bend one and crease it so badly that it will never work again.

✔ 5 1/4-inch drives may be a technology that's out of date, but having one in your computer (in addition to a 3 1/2-incher) has some

advantages. First, there are still skezillions of 5 1/4-inch diskettes in circulation, and it's nice to be able to read them—like when clients send you diskettes from their computer, or when your cousin gives you all his old software.

✔ Floppy disk drives can be either "high density" or "low density." High-density diskettes hold twice as much information, so you'll definitely want to get high-density disk drives, regardless of whether they're for 5 1/4-inch or 3 1/2-inch diskettes.

✔ High-density drives can use both high- and low-density diskettes. If you have a high-density disk drive, you should buy high-density diskettes to hold the maximum amount of information. You can also buy the less expensive low-density diskettes for when you don't need the diskette to hold so much.

✔ Having two disk drives is handy for making copies of diskettes—you can copy the contents of one directly onto the other, even though the diskettes are different sizes physically. Buying a PC with a second disk drive shouldn't add much—if anything—to its price. A top-quality floppy disk drive only costs about $75 retail.

✔ If your PC is going to have just one floppy disk drive, make it a 3 1/2-inch model. These diskettes are simply easier to handle and more durable than the 5 1/4-inch ones.

CAUTION

Don't be a cheapskate. Cheap diskettes are no bargain. You have to rely on a diskette to record faithfully and durably. Cheap diskettes can fail without warning, and one day when you put your crucial archive diskette into your computer, you might get the hair-raising message, "This disk is unreadable." Always buy diskettes with guarantees. Consider any higher

continues

continued

price you pay for good diskettes to be like an insurance policy—you may hate to do it, but it makes good sense.

"I HATE THIS!"

Hey! These diskettes are the wrong size!

A lot of PC programs are still sold on 5 1/4-inch diskettes so that they'll work on older machines. The day may come when you open a box of new software to discover that it contains a stack of 5 1/4-inch diskettes and a note that begins, "If you prefer 3 1/2-inch diskettes, please fill in the enclosed card...."

Mac Floppy Disk Drives

Mac buyers get no choices. They get the one disk drive that Apple builds in, and that's that. Love it or leave it.

A Macintosh disk drive can format diskettes to hold 800 kilobytes or 1.4 megabytes of information. In some Mac models, you also have the option of buying a "SuperDrive," which can read diskettes formatted by PCs. This capability can be very handy if some of your clients or coworkers use PCs. You won't be able to use PC programs, but you'll be able to read many PC-created files.

Hard Disks

Hard disks can hold much more information than diskettes, and they're mounted permanently inside the computer. Hard disks are indeed hard, like a phonograph record or compact disc, and they spin extremely fast.

They read and record information many times faster than a floppy disk drive.

The hard disk is where you'll keep the programs and work you frequently need. You really really really need one—and I mean each and every one of those "reallys."

The capacity of hard disks is rated in *megabytes*. The smallest hard disks you can buy (mainly used for laptop computers these days) have a capacity of 40 megabytes. The hard disks in desktop models start at 40 megabytes and range up into the hundreds of megabytes. Consider 80 megabytes the absolute minimum for your computer. The greater the capacity of the hard disk, the better. Believe me, no matter how much storage space you've got, you'll use it all.

EXPERTS ONLY

Big, really big, huge, gigantic disks!

A hard disk drive can contain several disks, stacked one on top of the other, each with its own read/record head. Stacking disks like this can give hard disk drives enormous capacities. You can be the first on your block to have a *gigabyte* (1000 megabytes) of hard disk storage—enough to put everybody in California on your Christmas card list.

CAUTION

The read/write head of a hard disk floats above the whizzing disk on a thin cushion of air. If the computer gets a sharp whack while the disk is spinning, the head tends to smack into the disk and take big divots out of it. This is called a *hard disk crash*, and it spells curtains for the information on the disk (and maybe for the disk itself). If you crash someone else's hard disk, it might be curtains for you, too.

I HATE BUYING A COMPUTER!

Yes, You Need One

Before you even ask, yes, you need a hard disk. You may never make a file any bigger than a three-page letter, but the programs you use need a hard disk.

Operating systems have gotten too big to fit on a floppy disk. My Macintosh operating system with all of the junk that goes along with it takes up 6 megabytes of hard disk space. The Windows operating system on my PC with its attendant baggage takes up almost 8 megabytes.

And application programs are just as bad. One of today's new pro- grams—with its tutorials, sample documents, dictionaries, thesauruses, "help" programs, and assorted bells and whistles—can take up 10 or 12 megabytes all by itself. Suddenly a 40-megabyte hard drive starts to feel a wee bit snug.

How Big Is Big Enough?

How big a hard disk you need depends on what you're going to use your computer for, but you shouldn't go any lower than 80 megabytes. Graph- ics files take up a lot of disk space. Desktop publishing files can be enor- mous. Programs that use moving pictures also take up gobs of disk space.

Fortunately, big hard drives are a bargain. Here are some sample prices for hard drives from a single manufacturer, pulled from a recent advertisement:

Capacity	Price
40 megabytes	$208
60 megabytes	$279
102 megabytes	$329
209 megabytes	$554

In other words, the price per megabyte drops really fast as disk size increases. For just $50 more than the cost of a 60-megabyte drive, you can get almost twice as much storage. That's a deal you can't afford to pass by.

TIP

If you're going to make a mistake about the size of the hard disk you buy, err on the high side—it's a much less costly error than buying a drive that's too small. A big hard disk will also enhance the resale value of the machine (assuming that you don't become so emotionally attached to it that you can never let go of it).

Hard Disk Speeds (Faster is better, again)

If you're planning on buying a Macintosh, you can skip this part—you don't get any choice about what kind of hard drive you get anyway. You'll get a good one, though, so don't worry.

Hard-disk manufacturers compete on the basis of how fast their drives work. These are the leading criteria you'll hear about when comparing hard disks:

▼ *Access Time*. This refers to how fast the read/record head can zip into position to pick up a particular piece of information from the disk. Anything less than 20 milliseconds (20/1,000 second) is fast enough. Beyond that, who's going to quibble about a few milliseconds? The time you lose dropping your pen on the floor wipes out all the milliseconds you saved in the last week with your TurboZip 500 BitWhiz Hard Drive.

▼ *Seek time*. This is the time it takes to move the recording head from point A to point B on the disk. But unlike access time, seek time leaves out the time it takes to scan the disk to find a particular piece of information. This makes it an unreliable indicator of how fast the drive will operate in real life. It fact, it's an utterly useless specification.

▼ *Transfer rate*. A better measure of a hard disk's efficiency is its transfer rate—the speed at which it can copy information off the disk and ship it to the computer's memory. A transfer rate of 5 megabytes per second is good, and 10 megabytes per second is really cookin'.

EXPERTS ONLY

Acronyms you don't need to know about

There's an avalanche of acronyms relating to how fast the hard drive can move the information it has found into your computer's memory, where it can be put to use. All of the following acronyms—ESDI, IDE, MFM, and SCSI—are synonymous with high-speed, high-performance, hard-drive technologies, and it's not necessary to know what any of them mean. But if you're curious, they're all in the glossary of buzzwords at the back of this book.

Memory

A computer has to have memory, but it's not like human memory, where we record things on a permanent basis (hopefully). Computer memory is short-term information storage.

All the computer's brain work is done in memory, which exists in the form of special microchips called *RAM* chips. In these chips, information is stored as an enormous array of tiny electrical charges. And these charges disappear in an instant if the power is cut off. In a computer, the line between genius and senility can be very thin.

BUZZWORDS

> **RAM**
>
> Computer engineers love acronyms. RAM is the name given to a computer's temporary-storage memory chips. It stands for "random-access memory," which sounds dysfunctional but somehow works anyway. Just remember that RAM—measured in kilobytes and megabytes—means *temporary* memory.

Memory for Programs

All computer programs work faster and more efficiently when your computer has plenty of memory.

Think back to a math professor calculating away at his blackboards. If on those blackboards he has all the information he needs to do his calculations, all he has to do to "access" that information is turn his head. If he has limited blackboard space, though, he'll have to keep some of that information somewhere else, perhaps in a notebook. Clearly, it's more

efficient for him to simply turn his head than to riffle through the pages of his notebook to find the data he wants.

It's the same for a computer. It works faster when it has a program in memory than when it has to read the program from a disk. When memory is limited, the computer has to spend time reading program instructions from the disk and putting them into memory where it can use them. When it needs additional instructions, it has to dump what it just put into memory so that it can make room for the new instructions it has to read from the disk. This constant read/write/erase/reread cycle can make programs run painfully slowly. And if a program is torturing you anyway, you don't want to prolong the agony.

The Measure of Memory

Computer memory is measured in megabytes. It used to be measured in kilobytes, but computers these days have more and more things on their minds.

As measures of capacity go, a megabyte is pretty abstract. Text, for instance, is pretty compact when stored on a computer, and a megabyte will hold about 700 pages of text. Color pictures, by comparison, contain so much information that 1 megabyte might not be enough to store a single baseball card.

How Much Memory Is Enough?

It's hard to say how much memory you need, but one thing is sure: what's enough today won't be enough next year. In 1984, the standard IBM PC and Macintosh came with 128 kilobytes of memory. By 1993, their operating systems alone—forget about other application programs—needed 2 megabytes of memory just to bring the computers to life. That's a 16-fold increase in required memory in less than 10 years.

The moral of this story? The phrase "too much memory" is a contradiction in terms.

Memory minimums

▼ If your PC is running DOS, you'll get by with 2 megabytes, but you'll be more comfortable with 4.

▼ If you run Windows, you should ignore Microsoft's 2-megabyte minimum. That's silly. You need at least 4 megabytes, and you should have 8.

▼ Macintoshes are happy with 4 megabytes, but more is better.

TIP

Make sure that your computer is built so that you can add more memory later, because future operating systems and programs are going to have bigger and bigger appetites for memory.

An Eye on the Future: Expanding Your Computer's Memory

Computers vary in the maximum amount of memory they can accommodate. Generally, when you buy a new computer, extra sockets are inside where you can plug in more memory chips, called *SIMMs*. Alternatively, you can plug larger-capacity chips into those sockets to achieve the same end.

I HATE BUYING A COMPUTER!

SIMMs

Nowadays, RAM comes in SIMMs. Say what? Single in-line memory modules, of course! In other words, you can add memory to your computer by simply plugging in more chips. There are other kinds of "plug-in memory," but SIMMs are the easiest to handle.

The capability to accommodate more memory isn't expensive, so look for a computer that can accept at least 16 megabytes of memory. Some models are limited to 4 or 8 megabytes, but if you're interested in the resale value of your machine, figure that in two years 8 megabytes might well be the absolute minimum that anyone would want.

TIP

It's no fun at all to try to add the memory yourself; it's a lot tougher than just plopping the new chips into your computer. If you want to expand your computer's memory, you should have a professional do it.

How Much Does Memory Cost?

The price of memory chips has declined steadily in recent years. In 1990 it was about $60 a megabyte for chips you could install yourself. By 1991 it had declined to about $45 a megabyte. And by 1993 it was down to around $35 a megabyte.

And that's retail. The folks who are building computers buy memory chips by the truckload, so the price they're paying is even lower. In other words, there's not much reason to put off buying memory until later when the prices go down (which they're apt to). Load up now and enjoy the luxury.

If the computer you're considering buying doesn't come with as much memory as you'd like, ask your computer dealer what they'd charge to add more memory for you. If you do this with a PC, remember to have them adjust the computer and it's operating system to accommodate the new memory—just plugging in the chips is not enough.

Remember this!

▼ Computers use two kinds of storage: temporary (memory) and permanent (disks).

▼ Hard disk drives are typically built into the computer and are used for storing very large amounts of information. Floppy disk drives have removable diskettes for saving smaller amounts of information.

▼ PCs can use 5 1/4-inch or 3 1/2-inch diskettes, or both. Macs use only 3 1/2-inch diskettes.

▼ Different kinds of diskettes hold different amounts of information.

▼ Hard disks come in various capacities, and megabytes of hard disk storage are cheaper by the dozen. Much cheaper.

▼ It's much better to buy a hard disk with a capacity that's too big than too small.

▼ A computer uses its memory—commonly called *RAM*—as a scratch pad for doing its many calculations.

▼ How much memory your computer needs depends on the application programs you run. For most popular computer systems, 4 megabytes is a practical minimum.

CHAPTER 9

Monitors
(I Can See Clearly Now)

IN A NUTSHELL

▼ Letting your eyes be the judge

▼ Pixels, video memory, and refresh rates

▼ Mac and PC display standards

▼ How big a monitor is big enough?

▼ Resolution issues

▼ The case for black and white

▼ Gray-scale monitors

▼ The glory of living color

▼ Monitor bundles

▼ The importance of knobs

▼ Health issues

I HATE BUYING A COMPUTER!

Buying a computer monitor is where sense—your sense of vision, that is—triumphs over science. When you're buying a monitor, remember this: no wealth of statistics or technical specifications can tell you that something looks good when it doesn't. You're going to be gazing into your computer's screen for untold hours, so you'd better like what you see.

In this chapter, you'll learn the buying criteria for computer monitors: both the visual and the technical. You almost always have a choice of monitors when you're buying a computer, and since it's the part of the computer you're trusting your eyes to, it's a very important choice indeed.

CAUTION

Yes, you CAN louse up your eyesight by sitting in front of a computer. (Remember what Mom used to say about sitting too close to the TV?) This happens mainly when the image on the monitor isn't clear and sharp enough. If the image is soft or fuzzy, your eyes will wage a constant and losing battle to draw a focus. This causes eyestrain, headaches, irritability, and the alienation of your coworkers and family.

The Eyes Have It

What do you look for when you're buying a monitor? Just a few things:

▼ A stable image—no fluttering, quivering, or shimmering.

▼ A clear, focused image in all parts of the screen, even the corners.

▼ A perfectly rectangular screen image—no warping or bulging at the corners or sides.

▼ A non-glare surface; you shouldn't see your own reflection staring back at you.

In short, you're looking for something that looks as much as possible like a printed page. After you've looked at a few monitors, you'll realize that this seemingly simple list of criteria is really pretty difficult to match.

The Man behind the Screen

The monitor of a computer is dumb. It makes nice pictures, but it doesn't have any brains. It only follows orders given to it by a chip-encrusted circuit board—called a *display adapter*—that's mounted inside the computer.

The job of the display adapter is to take instructions from your programs and adapt them into an image composed of dots that can be displayed on your monitor. If the image is soft or fuzzy, it's not the adapter's fault; the adapter just describes the image. The monitor makes that image visible, for better or worse.

Not all display adapters work alike, and not all monitors work alike. Some display adapters work only with a specific brand-name monitor; some work with many brands. You can buy a matched pair, or you can buy the adapter and the monitor separately. Just remember that it takes two to tango.

A Teaspoon of Technology

Here's how your computer, display adapter, and monitor work together, in three painless paragraphs (not counting this one). Knowing this process will make sense out of almost anything a computer ad or salesperson has to say on the subject.

1. The computer sends information to the display adapter, which builds its pictures in memory before it sends them to the screen—the more complex the image, the more memory the display adapter needs.

2. The display adapter sends the information to the monitor and re-draws the screen several times every second, which enables things to appear to move and change smoothly when you're working on your computer. A TV set does the same thing so that the cops running across the screen aren't moving all herky-jerky.

3. The monitor displays a picture made up of dots, called *pixels* (short for *picture elements*). The smaller these dots are, the sharper the image.

EXPERTS ONLY

A lecturette on screen resolution

The smallness of the dots on a computer monitor is measured by how many of them fit in a given area, and this figure is called the *resolution* of the screen. Macintosh screen resolutions are measured in pixels per inch (the norm, for instance, is 72 pixels per inch), whereas PC resolutions are defined by how many pixels fit on the whole screen (typically 640 pixels horizontally by 480 pixels vertically).

✔ Most standard computers these days come with a VGA display adapter. This means that your computer is capable of displaying color and will take care of all your displaying needs. Very few people will need more than this. You'll learn more about VGA later in this chapter, so consider this just a sneak preview.

✔ If you need to use your computer to run Windows, you might need a display adapter with extra memory. For instance, a display adapter with 1 megabyte of memory can handle complex images more quickly than a display adapter with only 1/2 megabyte of memory.

BUZZWORDS

REFRESH RATE

To keep the screen consistently bright, the display adapter continuously rebuilds—or refreshes—the image. The number of times this happens per second is called the *refresh rate*. Allegedly, higher refresh rates are better, but this specification is absolutely no predictor of image quality.

Display Standards

A *display standard* is nothing more than a method of creating screen images that has been accepted by a broad segment of the computer industry. Through the years, several display standards have come and gone. The most popular offerings in the current crop are VGA and Super VGA. Here's what you need to know about them.

VGA (Common denominator color)

VGA is far and away the most common display standard for PCs these days, and it's a very good one. VGA stands for *Video Graphics Array*, and a VGA picture measures 640 pixels horizontally by 480 pixels vertically. This translates to about 75 pixels per inch on a typical PC screen. VGA images can be in color or black and white.

On a typical PC screen of 12 or 13 inches, VGA provides resolution that's almost exactly the same as on a Macintosh. And like the Mac, VGA gives you a choice of how many colors you want to display. All modern software supports VGA, so you're safe with this choice.

TIP

An important thing to remember is that a monitor can adhere to a standard but execute it badly. For this reason, you should never buy a monitor sight unseen. Standards cannot create quality.

Super VGA to the Rescue! (More colors, higher resolution: Up, up, and away!)

It's very common for monitors and display adapters to offer what's called *Super* VGA. Although the VGA was invented and defined by IBM, the Super VGA standard was designed by consensus; a lot of companies started making higher-than-VGA-resolution monitors, and they became known collectively as Super VGA.

The most common Super VGA resolutions are 800 by 600 pixels and 1,024 by 768 pixels. Many VGA systems can also display at Super VGA resolutions. The 800-by-600 resolution looks good on a 13- or 14-inch screen, but to be effective, the 1,024-by-768 resolution needs a larger

screen (15 inches and up). On screens smaller than 15 inches, the smaller pixels at the 1,024-by-768 resolution make many screen details too small to be seen well.

EXPERTS ONLY

XGA marks the spot

The latest PC display standard again comes from IBM (for a struggling company, they still have a lot of good ideas). It's called XGA, for Extended Graphic Array. Made for large screens of 19 inches and up, it specifies a resolution of 1,280 pixels horizontally by 1,024 pixels vertically.

CAUTION

Avoid PC systems that can use only out-of-date display standards such as MDA (Monochrome Display Adapter), CGA (Color Graphics Adapter), or EGA (Enhanced Graphics Adapter). You want VGA or Super VGA.

Macintosh Display Standards

On the Apple side of the fence, all Macintosh monitors either (a) support the basic Apple display standard or (b) come with their own special display adapter that creates some custom resolution. If you're intent on buying a Mac, that's all you need to know. You can skip ahead to the next section. PC shoppers, keep reading; as usual, you've got more choices.

Choosing the Right Monitor for You

There may be a lot of monitors out there, but there are only a few basic questions you need to answer to trim down the list. In semilogical order, they are:

▼ What screen size do you want?

▼ Do you want a color or black-and-white monitor?

▼ If it's color, how many colors do you want?

Size Isn't Everything

Computer monitors are measured like TV sets: diagonally. And like TV sets, the image that appears on them doesn't completely fill the screen. The image on my 13-inch Macintosh monitor, for example, is actually only a little over 11 inches, and the image on my 15-inch PC monitor is really only a little over 12 inches. In other words, my PC's nominal 2-inch advantage doesn't add up to much in real life. When you go shopping for a monitor, bring a tape measure.

Bigger screens are luxurious, like big beds are luxurious—you get plenty of elbow room. If you're creating graphics, you can see more of your image on a bigger screen. If you're editing text, you can see more lines, although on most screens, you get to see only about half a page at a time.

Full-page monitors or double-page monitors (about the size of 19-inch TVs) are great for professionals. Professional word processors, for example, will welcome the ability to see an entire 8 1/2-by-11-inch page on-screen at one time. And desktop publishers will appreciate being able to see complete composed pages at life size.

TIP

Full-page monitors are expensive. As a rule of thumb, figure that a monitor that measures twice as large as a normal one will cost four times as much because the image it creates is four times larger. A bigger monitor needs a bigger picture tube and a much more complex display adapter with a ton of memory to create an image so big. You're paying by the pixel.

But ultimately, the size of the screen isn't as important as the clarity of its image. It's always a better deal to trade a slightly larger screen for a smaller, clearer one of the same price.

Checklist

✔ All computer programs support VGA, but not all are equipped to support Super VGA, which means you might not get the extra benefits you paid for. If the main reason you're considering Super VGA is to use it with a certain program, make sure that program is equipped to use it.

✔ If you plan to use just DOS programs, a 14-inch monitor with a VGA adapter will do just fine for you. Anything else is overkill.

✔ If you plan to use Windows programs—and especially if you expect to use more than one Windows program at once—a 15-inch or larger monitor may well be worth the extra cost.

✔ Whatever you do, don't get an interlaced Super VGA monitor. You'll get a truly annoying flickery image in graphics mode.

The Case for Black and White

If you haven't been around computers for a while, you'll be happy to know that green letters on a black background have been relegated to the dustbin of history. The unnecessarily highfalutin term *monochrome* can now do the same. State-of-the-art monochrome monitors are now good old black and white.

With today's black-and-white monitors, you have the choice of displaying your work as white on a black background or as black on a white background—the way we normally see printed pages.

But it's getting harder and harder to find a simple black-and-white monitor these days. Color computer displays are just the cat's pajamas.

"I HATE THIS!"

You can't live without a color monitor. Not!

Despite what marketers say, computer screen color is gratuitous and decorative in most programs. It doesn't help distinguish things on-screen, and it isn't easier on the eyes— in fact, quite the contrary. A true black-and-white screen (as opposed to a color screen displaying in black and white) has a sharper image than a color monitor. Anyone who tells you differently is probably trying to sell you a color monitor.

In Living Color

Almost every monitor you see these days is color. Computers use color for two reasons. One is to display the colors you create yourself in an

application program, such as the colors you add to a pie chart or graph in a graphics program—in other words, color you can print (assuming that you've got a color printer).

The other reason computers use color is to present programs more dramatically or effectively. The Macintosh operating system, for example, lets you color-code file icons; that way you can see at a glance which files need urgent attention, which ones came from someone else's computer, and so on. A lot of computer color, though, is just decoration.

How Many Colors Are Enough?

How many colors you want displayed on-screen depends on what kind of work you do. On the current generation of PCs, the minimum number of colors you can display is 16, in the normal VGA standard. If you mostly work with text and bar charts, that's plenty. You don't need any more than that unless you plan to work with color photographs or color desktop publishing on your computer.

If you add more video memory to your PC display adapter, the number of colors you can display jumps up to 256, 32,000, 64,000, or 16.7 million, a number normally reserved for professional graphic artists creating slick magazine images, for example, or professional video productions. On Macs, you can choose between 256 and 16.7 million colors. 256 colors on a computer screen looks like a super TV image. The image on a screen that can display 16.7 million looks like a color photograph.

A color Macintosh monitor or a color VGA screen for a PC has the potential to display 16.7 million colors—how many you actually see depends on the display adapter you buy and on how much memory is built into it.

I HATE BUYING A COMPUTER!

EXPERTS ONLY

A little bit about color

The number of colors a monitor can produce is often identified by the number of bits of information the computer dedicates to describing the color of each pixel. If it uses just 1 bit, the monitor can display only black or white. If it uses 8 bits, the monitor can display 256 tones, either grays or colors. 24-bit color—used by professional graphic artists and video editors—can create 16.7 million colors. There aren't enough pixels on-screen to show all these colors at once, but your programs can pick from this enormous range of hues when displaying images.

Measuring Resolution

The resolution of PC monitors is typically expressed in how many pixels fit on the screen. VGA—the most common current PC display standard—has a resolution of 640 pixels horizontally by 480 pixels vertically. Buying a bigger VGA screen, then, doesn't necessarily give you a wider window; you still get 640 by 480—the pixels are just larger. You're right, that's dumb. Making the pixels bigger just makes images look jaggier and cruder; you're just making the bricks bigger. The reason for buying a bigger screen is to see *more* things, not to see the same things bigger.

On a PC, if you want a wider view of your work, you have to buy a display adapter that actually puts more pixels on the screen.

"I HATE THIS!"

Dot pitch, schmot pitch!

Computer salespeople might try to confuse you with a term called "dot pitch," a useless specification that relates to the size of screen pixels and how closely they're spaced on a computer screen. Dot pitch is no more a predictor of how good a monitor looks than your height is a predictor of how good a basketball player you are.

Monitors and Display Adapters (Arranged marriages)

On the Macintosh, most monitors come with their own display adapters—the two are made for each other and have to be used together. The Mac operating system is smart enough to know what's going on and adjusts itself to the new hardware.

On the PC, you can buy a display adapter from one company and a monitor from another. In fact, this is the typical arrangement, which means that you (or, much better, someone else) will have to adjust one to the other and then tell the operating system what's going on so that the display adapter, monitor, and operating system all work together. It's more complicated than on a Mac, but once it's set up, you never have to worry about it again. Whoever sells you your computer should do this setting up for you.

TIP

Always ask what other standards your PC's display adapter will work with. If you think you might want higher-than-VGA resolution at some later date, for instance, ask whether it can also display Super VGA or XGA images. If you think you might want more colors, find out how many colors the display adapter can potentially create and how much it will cost to add the additional video memory that displaying them requires.

Knobs

Like TV sets, monitors have contrast and brightness controls. These should be located somewhere around the front of the monitor where you can reach them easily.

Color monitors, however, typically do not have color controls. For applications where precise color is crucial, such as electronically retouching photographs, you can control the colors of the display from within your application program.

Some monitors add lots of other knobs that let you control the width of the image on the screen, or its height, or how well it's centered on the screen. These knobs are essentially worthless. If the screen has been properly calibrated in the factory, all these things should be just fine when you buy it.

EXPERTS ONLY

Want your colors to be their brightest?
If you're concerned about accurate on-screen color, your monitor should also have—are you ready for this?—

a "de-gaussing button." A *gauss* (which rhymes with *louse*) is a measure of magnetic fields that, in the case of monitors (especially color ones), accumulate while the computer is turned on. A surplus of gausses causes the colors on your screen to look washed out. Pushing the de-gaussing button chases away all the bad gausses, so your colors look their brightest.

Health Issues

Ever since personal computers were invented, people have worried about the health consequences of being parked in front of one, hour after hour, day after day. The jury is still out on the risks of being a career computer jockey. I, for one, feel fine—though all my hair has recently turned green and I'm sprouting what appears to be a third arm. Just kidding.

The Debatable Problems

The images on your screen are created by a stream of electrons that make a special coating of chemicals glow just behind the glass that's a foot or two in front of your nose. In other words, that stream of electrons is aimed right at your face.

Computer monitors give off a low level of magnetic radiation, but this is not the same kind of radiation that comes from atomic weapons or nuclear plants. Studies on the health effects of sitting in front of a computer screen for prolonged periods have been contradictory, but by and large they have failed to identify monitor radiation as a source of malady

or disease. A computer's radio emissions are controlled by government standards, for whatever that's worth.

Definite Problems with Definite Solutions

The more likely health problems caused by monitors are stiff necks, from having the screen mounted too high or too low, and eyestrain, from screens with fuzzy images and from spending too long with your eyes focused at the same fixed distance. It's important to look away from your computer from time to time to allow your eyes to relax by focusing at various, longer distances. Try taking a walk to the water cooler.

Studies have also shown that while people are gazing into computer monitors, they tend to blink less often and their eyeballs dry out (I'm serious!), which can cause particular problems for contact lens wearers. The fact that you have to be reminded to keep blinking is a measure of the hypnotic effect of these machines.

Checklist

✔ For glasses wearers who spend a lot of time at a computer, opticians often recommend slightly tinted lenses.

✔ Your monitor should not be facing a light source, such as a window or lamp. This causes glare, which is hard on your eyes.

✔ If your monitor is sitting so low that you have to bow your head, raise the monitor by putting a couple of old phone books (or unwieldy computer books) beneath it.

✔ Some people find that overhead fluorescent lights hurt their eyes when using a computer. You might want to try a halogen lamp.

I HATE BUYING A COMPUTER!

Remember this!

▼ Your eyes are the best judge of the quality of a monitor's image. No avalanche of impressive specifications and statistics can contradict what you see with your own eyes.

▼ Your computer's display system consists of two parts: the monitor, and a display adapter board that mounts inside your computer. The adapter defines the images, and the monitor displays them.

▼ Display adapters build your monitor's images in memory. The more complex the images (for example, the more colors they contain), the more memory the adapter needs. The more memory the adapter contains, the more expensive it is.

▼ A single monitor can work with many display adapters, and vice versa.

▼ The higher the resolution—that is, the more dots per inch that are used to create the monitor's image—the smoother the image will be. The more dots you display on-screen, the more memory the display adapter needs.

▼ Black-and-white monitors are easier on the eyes than color monitors.

▼ Color monitors can display anywhere from 16 to 16 million colors.

▼ Monitors and display adapters are often bundled together.

▼ There is no conclusive proof that the radio emissions given off by monitors are bad for your health.

CHAPTER 10

Buses, Ports, and Input Devices
(Ins, Outs, and Assorted Connections)

IN A NUTSHELL

- ▼ How information gets through a computer
- ▼ What a computer bus is
- ▼ Expansion boards for new capabilities
- ▼ Serial, parallel, and SCSI connections
- ▼ Keyboards and mice

When you're buying a computer, you have to make three decisions regarding what's probably the most complicated technical aspect of the computer. These decisions are the following:

▼ What kind of bus do you want?

▼ Which communications ports do you want?

▼ Which kind of keyboard and mouse do you want?

This chapter gives you all the information you need to make these decisions intelligently and easily. And after your computer is up and running, you'll probably never have to think about this stuff again.

How Information Gets Through a Computer

All three of the decisions mentioned earlier relate to how information flows through a computer. In the tongue of the trade, this information flow is generically referred to as input/output, or I/O.

To understand this concept, think of the computer as an information pump. It draws information through sockets called communications *ports*. Your keyboard attaches to a port, for example.

When the information is inside the computer, it travels around through an electronic plumbing system called a *bus*. The bus connects the disk drives, the communications ports, and all the other assorted whatchamacallits inside the computer.

And just as the bus has entrances, it also has exits (also called ports), through which the computer squirts the information back out again—to a printer, for example. The more efficient the pumping, the faster the computer runs.

Are You on the Right Bus?

Although there's a lot of talk about computer buses these days, especially PC buses, you really only need to know two things about your computer's bus: how much information can get through it at one time, and how many other gizmos you can plug into it.

Bus Choice #1: Wide Pipes or Narrow Pipes?

Some buses have pipes (data paths) that are only wide enough to handle 16 bits of information at a time. But today's insanely powerful microprocessors can pump 32 bits of information at a time. If you have a narrow-pipe bus and a wide-pipe microprocessor, you'll have inefficient pumping, clogged pipes, and information backing up and spilling all over your desk. Okay, I'm exaggerating—but what's the point of having a high-speed pump fed by tiny pipes?

The bottom line: You want a 32-bit plumbing system, a 32-bit bus.

EXPERTS ONLY

Bus Standards

PCs have several types of buses, called *bus standards*, which are identified (naturally) by abbreviations. Here's a rundown on the most popular ones and how wide their data pipes are:

EISA (Extended System Standard Architecture)	32 bits
ISA (Industry Standard Architecture)	16 bits
MCA (MicroChannel Architecture, IBM only)	16 or 32 bits

Bus Choice #2: How Many Expansion Slots?

The second thing you need to know about buses is that they come with sockets into which you can plug other gizmos that give your computer new capabilities. These sockets are called *expansion slots*. The things you plug into them—circuit boards filled with chips and electronic what-have-you—are called expansion boards, or add-on cards, or add-in boards, or something similar.

Things you might plug into an expansion slot

▼ The display adapter for your monitor

▼ An internal modem

▼ A network card so that you can connect your computer to a network of other computers

▼ A sound card so that you can produce cool special effects

Having a lot of expansion slots in your computer adds to its cost and makes it take up more desk space. Although you could get so many peripherals that you run out of expansion slots, most people don't use more than three or four.

TIP

Expansion boards only work with the bus for which they were designed. Both PCs and Macs have different kinds of buses—different bus standards—no one of which has any great practical advantage over any other (apart from the width of its data paths).

BUZZWORDS

LOCAL BUS VIDEO

More and more computer manufacturers use standard buses, but customize one part: the information pipe that leads from the microprocessor to the monitor's display adapter. This pipe is called local bus video, and it speeds up the display of information on your computer's screen.

Communications Ports

Communications ports are like the plugs on the back of a stereo amplifier. There's one port for the cassette player to plug in, another for the radio tuner, another for the record player (if you still own one), and so forth.

In the same way, you use computer ports to attach some device, like a printer, a keyboard, or a mouse, to your computer.

Types of ports

▼ **Serial:** Serial connections are typically used to link computers to telephone lines and to other computers.

▼ **Parallel:** Parallel ports are popular for connecting computers to printers. Parallel connections play limited roles, though, because they can't reach very far, only a few feet.

▼ **Bus:** Bus ports are used for connecting the keyboard and mouse to the computer. Many PCs, though, use a serial port for connecting the mouse, which is really a waste of a perfectly good serial port.

continues

I HATE BUYING A COMPUTER!

Types of ports (continued)

▼ **SCSI:** SCSI is pronounced "scuzzy." SCSI connections are popular for linking hardware devices on Macintoshes. They're used, for instance, to connect computers to printers, scanners, and external hard disks. Very few PCs use SCSI ports.

TIP

For every communications port, there's a cable with the same name. You need a serial cable, then, to connect to a serial port to perform a serial communication. Cables are cheap, but many computer dealers are even cheaper. Make sure they supply you with all the cables you need, especially when you're buying a printer.

TIP

In a PC, one parallel and two serial ports is the minimum arrangement you should accept. This configuration is enough to accommodate a parallel printer, a serial mouse, and a serial telephone connection. If you want to add other devices, you may have to add more ports. An expansion board with another parallel port and two more serial ports costs less than $50.

You as Input Device

Most of the valuable information that goes into the computer is put there by you, tapping away at the keyboard and mousing around with your mouse. The following sections describe your options when purchasing these input tools.

Keyboards

You don't get much choice here; most keyboards are pretty much the same. They have the basic typewriter keys plus a row of function keys (mainly used for issuing program commands at the stroke of a button) and a numeric keypad that looks like the keys from an adding machine.

Things to look for when buying keyboards

▼ Keyboards may all look the same, but they can feel different. If possible, spend some time typing at the keyboard before you buy a computer.

▼ Some keyboards have better tactile response than others. With some keyboards, it's hard to tell whether you've pressed the keys hard enough. With good keyboards, you can hear a slight click when the key connects, which makes for faster touch typing.

▼ The keyboard should be heavy so that it doesn't slide around when you start typing fast.

▼ Some keyboards have function keys along the top of the keyboard; others have function keys along the left. Most people prefer them along the top.

▼ For a demonstration of a good keyboard, try out any IBM computer. They've been in the keyboard-making business longer than anybody.

EXPERTS ONLY

My fingers are cramped!

Laptop computers can only have a keyboard as wide as your lap, so they have fewer keys than full-size computers. Laptops don't have a numeric keypad and have fewer function keys.

CHAPTER 10

TIP

When you're shopping for a PC, you may be able to negotiate for a different keyboard if it's the only aspect of a particular computer that you don't like. Keyboards are standardized, and you can usually swap them without a problem.

Mice

On the PC, you can buy two- or three-button mice. Most programs only use one of these buttons. Microsoft manufactures the most popular mouse (that is, the one that most computer sellers bundle with their systems).

Like a PC printer or a PC monitor, a PC mouse needs a driver (a program that tells your computer's other programs how the mouse works). When you buy your system, get your dealer to install the mouse driver for you.

Mice have different feels. Some slide better than others, for example. Make sure you try the mouse out before you buy the computer. You want to get one that's comfortable for you.

Things to consider when buying a mouse

▼ If you're going to get a mouse, get a mouse pad, too. Your mouse will move more smoothly if you roll it on the mouse pad instead of your desk.

▼ Some mice are a little bit heavier than others; a mouse that's a little heavier is actually easier to maneuver precisely.

▼ Trackballs are a different kind of mouse, where you move the pointer by spinning a stationary ball. Trackballs are good for desks that are tight on space and don't have room to roll a mouse around.

▼ If you're going to get a Macintosh, you don't have to worry about buying a mouse because your Mac will have one included.

CHAPTER 11

Buying a Portable Computer
(Take Me Along)

IN A NUTSHELL

- ▼ Portables vs. laptops
- ▼ Sacrifices for portability
- ▼ Laptop-buyer's checklist
- ▼ Durability issues

In general, you shop for a portable computer just like you shop for a desktop model. After all, a portable should be able to run all the same programs and do all the same things as its bigger sibling. Portables just do them, well, smaller.

This chapter covers what you gain and lose by buying a portable computer and the special considerations involved with buying one of these wee wonders.

"I HATE THIS!"

Where'd I put that #%$@ PC?!

When you buy a portable computer, you gain only one thing: portability. In exchange, you get a smaller screen, a smaller keyboard, a higher price tag, and the possibility that you'll leave your computer under the table at a restaurant. This last little inconvenience is much less likely to happen with your desktop model.

Two Kinds of Portability

You can divide the various kinds of portable computers into two types:

▼ *Portables*, which have a handle, get toted like a piece of luggage and have to be plugged into the wall. (Some portables can run on batteries, but not for long enough to be considered for anything but emergency backup.)

▼ *Laptops* (including so-called *notebook* computers) are light in weight, fold in half like a wallet, and can either run on batteries or be plugged into a wall socket.

Portables (If only barely)

Portable computers, like portable TVs, get their name because they have a handle on top. The handle is strong enough to lift the thing, but you may not be. Hence, these little puppies are often referred to as *luggables*. In other words, they're not something you want to have in tow as you make a mad dash through the airport.

A portable's portability is based on having its monitor, CPU, and (usually) the keyboard in one unit. The keyboard is typically hinged to the rest of the unit and simply folds down into position.

Falling between desktop model and laptop, portables generally combine the worst of both worlds. If you want a really portable PC, buy a laptop. If you want a good desktop machine with a nice big screen, buy a traditional console model.

Because they're really crummy, luggables seem to be going the way of the dinosaur. Don't get one.

Laptops and Notebooks

A laptop computer is, sensibly enough, a computer that fits on your lap...without crushing your knees or giving you shin splints. They generally weigh less than 10 pounds.

A notebook computer is a smaller version of a laptop, and it's often difficult to tell one from the other without reading what's printed on the box. In principle, a notebook computer should fit inside a businessperson's attaché case and weigh in at less than 8 pounds. Anything I say here about laptops applies to notebook computers as well.

"I HATE THIS!"

Fanatical reasons why you shouldn't get a laptop

Laptop computers are cute. They're compact. They're portable. They're tyrannical. When you have a laptop computer, it's like having a harpy hovering over your head, always whining, "Why aren't you working?!" In your car, at the bus stop, on the airplane, in the john—all your old safe havens from work are no longer secure. We *need* excuses to spend unproductive moments, but laptop computers are taking them away from us. And when I'm in charge....

Sorry about that. It's just that laptops push a political button for me. I *like* to be able to walk away from my work. I *like* staring idly out the airplane window. I *like* sitting on the beach without working on a spreadsheet.

What you give up for portability

▼ A *decent screen display*. Laptop screens are small, only two-thirds or less the height of a standard computer screen. And narrower to boot. A smaller view of your work is a liability. This is especially true for spreadsheets, where you want to see as many rows and columns at once as possible.

Laptop screens are also harder to look at than standard monitors. A standard desktop monitor gives you a nice bright picture that's easy on the eyeballs. Laptop screens use liquid-crystal displays that can be hard to see well in certain lighting conditions.

▼ A *full-size keyboard*. Because laptop and notebook computers are smaller than normal computers, their keyboards are often smaller also. You can get used to these miniaturized keyboards, but it's gonna take a little work.

▼ *Comfortable posture.* A laptop's keyboard is hinged to its monitor. Wherever the keyboard goes, the monitor has to follow. If you watch people using laptop computers, you'll notice that they tend to lean into their work to get a better view of the screen. The taller you are, the worse the problem. This might work on an airplane, but you don't want to work this way as a matter of course.

TIP

Consider a laptop as your second computer. Unless you really positively gotta have portability.

BUZZWORDS

LCD

LCD stands for *liquid crystal display.* An LCD display consists of a very fine grid, each square of which contains a magic chemical that can be made opaque or clear by a burst of electricity. It's the same principal as digital watches, only much larger. Laptop and notebook computers use LCD screens because they're light, thin, and don't use much electricity.

Things To Watch for

Laptop computer shoppers have some particular considerations that regular computer shoppers don't. Some—like batteries—are concerns unique to laptops. Others are items that are implemented differently on laptops, so they need your special attention. In general, shop for a laptop like you'd shop for a desktop computer, but with the following additional considerations.

Batteries (Power by the pound)

Much of the weight of a portable computer is its rechargeable batteries. The weight of the batteries is a convenience issue. How long they'll hold a charge is a more important consideration.

The two most popular kinds of laptop computer batteries are *nickel-cadmium* (a.k.a., *NiCad*) and *nickel-metal-hydride* (a.k.a., *nickel-metal-hydride*). Nickel-cadmium batteries are cheaper and don't hold a charge for quite as long as nickel-metal-hydride batteries. In fact, they're so much cheaper that most portable-computer buyers opt for nickel-cadmium.

TIP

When you're buying a laptop, bargain for a great deal on a second set of batteries and an external battery recharger. That way, while one set of batteries is recharging, you can keep working by using the others. The second set of batteries will come in handy during long flights.

Laptop computer batteries do not hold a charge for very long. Despite clever technologies to extend battery life (the equivalent of coasting out of gear in your car), a fully charged battery may give you less than three hours of work time. Then you have to recharge the batteries by plugging the unit into the wall.

Levels of candor vary about how long a battery will hold a charge. Six hours is, by consensus, stretching the limits of credulity. A really good battery lasts for around four hours.

Ways to save battery power

▼ Don't turn the backlighting up any higher than is necessary to see clearly. Notebook backlighting drains energy quickly—the brighter, the faster.

▼ Use power management software. Almost all laptops and notebooks come with special software that monitors how long each part of the computer has been inactive. If a part has been inactive for a while, it shuts down until you need it again. This kind of software can significantly increase the life of your batteries.

Weight (Passive body building)

No matter how little your notebook or laptop seems to weigh when you heft it around in the store, the computer magically doubles in weight when you're carrying it around in the JFK airport.

Still, weight should be fairly low on your priorities list. Your primary concerns are function and durability. And durability—including shock resistance—often comes with a little extra heft.

Things to make your laptop heavier

When you take a notebook or laptop on the road, you never take *just* the computer. You're going to need to bring along some peripherals, like these:

▼ A *carrying case*. Many portable computers come with their own special padded case, which can guard against the shock of traveling.

▼ AC *adapter*. You'll want to be able to recharge the computer once its batteries are drained.

continues

▼ *Extra batteries*. If you own extra batteries, bring them. More than likely, you'll need them.

▼ *Disks*, *manuals*, *cables*. The junk that collects around your computer sometimes has to go on the road with you.

Screen Quality

Laptop screens are not bright enough. They can't be, or they'd suck the batteries dry in two minutes flat.

Most laptops use liquid-crystal displays (LCD) that come in color or black-and-white. They're flat, they're lightweight, and the bad ones can drive your eyes goo-goo. Even good ones aren't all that great.

Color laptop displays cost a lot—more than they're worth, unless you absolutely *must* have color. Color is not only a drain on your budget, it's also an extra drain on your precious batteries.

EXPERTS ONLY

Backlit or side-lit: That is the question

Laptop LCD screens are illuminated in one of two ways. *Backlit* screens are just that: lit from the back, with the light that comes through the shutters being located directly behind them. *Side-lit* screens are illuminated obliquely from the edges of the screen. You're right, this isn't as efficient, and side-lit screens aren't as bright as back-lit screens. But they're cheaper, and they don't exhaust the batteries as fast.

TIP

When you shop for a laptop, insist on having it demonstrated in real-life conditions. Not in a softly lit show room, but next to a bright window or in the back seat of a car. You want a screen that you can read easily in all conditions. Otherwise, you may wind up on the plane using your in-flight blanket as a tent for viewing the weak light trickling from your laptop's screen.

Hard Disk Size

Portable means dropable. The hard-disk drives in portable computers are rugged, but they still can't take much abuse. This means you're probably not going to be storing a lot of stuff on your hard disk. One false move, and—kablooey!—it all goes to data heaven.

Unless you have some huge database that you need to carry around with you, you're better off with a modest-size disk drive of 40 or 80 megabytes—enough to fit your operating system and the application programs you intend to use. Carry your valuable data files on floppy disks.

Floppy Disk Drives

You want one. You need one. One that can use high-density (1+ megabyte) floppy disks. It's the best way to get work off your laptop and onto your desktop. And vice versa.

Connections

The main use of laptop computers is to allow people to keep working while they're away from their desktop computers. This means that when

they get back to their desks, they have to get their new work off the laptop and on to their main computer.

By far the best way to accomplish this feat is with floppy disks. But if you have to transfer larger files—databases, for instance—you'll need a special program made specifically for linking portable and desktop computers. These programs typically use standard cables to link the two computers. Many notebook computers come with a copy of this type of program. Ask the salesperson.

Durability

How tough are portable computers? Because laptops haven't been around very long, this question is unanswerable. Fortunately, you don't need to reckon with this query when you're shopping for a desktop computer—unless you're a very, very rough typist.

Bouncing is the most obvious trial to confront a laptop. As you might suspect, laptops do not bounce well. They jostle okay, and can bump and clunk occasionally without damage. But one good whack can do them in.

TIP

When you're comparing laptops, also compare the carrying cases that accompany them. Some are sturdy padded affairs, and others are mere slip covers. After you determine how a good one looks, bargain with your dealer to throw in a good one when you buy your laptop.

A less obvious problem with laptops is heat. Computer components can't take the heat—and they give off lots of it—but they can't get out of the kitchen. Desktop computers have a built-in fan to keep things

cool, but laptops have no fans. Some early laptop models even suffered meltdowns—they got so hot that some of their innards melted.

So while desktop computers have been around long enough to be able to guarantee some kind of longevity (they're amazingly durable), the jury is still out on laptops.

TIP

Even if you don't plan to use your laptop during a flight, don't check it in with your luggage—too great a chance of the laptop being broken. Keep your laptop as a carry on.

Remember this!

▼ If you get a laptop, get it for your *second* computer. Desktop models are a much better deal unless you really need portability.

▼ Battery life—the longer the better, but remember that battery-life claims may not reflect real-life situations. Ask the salesperson, "How long will the battery last if I'm doing such-and-such kind of work?"

▼ Screen quality—the better the better. Examine the screen in real-life lighting situations. Unlike with your desktop model, you won't always have control over the lighting in the places you're using your laptop.

▼ Storage—you want a high-density floppy disk drive and medium-size hard disk.

▼ Weight—all other things being equal, opt for the lighter model, but remember that the weight you have to carry will be more than the weight of the computer by itself. You have to carry the carrying case, extra batteries, charging cables, disks, and so on.

CHAPTER 12

Printers
(Getting It down on Paper)

IN A NUTSHELL

- ▼ Dot-matrix printers
- ▼ Lasers and laser-like printers
- ▼ Inkjet printers
- ▼ Color printers
- ▼ All about fonts
- ▼ Speed, memory, expansions, and connections
- ▼ Prices and per-page costs

I HATE BUYING A COMPUTER!

Buying a printer is probably more complicated than buying a computer. (I'm sure you're happy to hear that little bit of news.) With a computer, you have only two basic options—Mac or PC—and the rest is quibbling about options. But with printers, you can choose from about half a dozen basic kinds. And then there are the brands and the options and the colors and....

This chapter cuts this onerous task down to size by answering two simple questions:

▼ How nice do you want your pages to look?

▼ How fast do you want your pages to print?

After you've answered those questions, we can talk about things like how easy particular printers are to use and how much you want to spend.

Dot-Matrix Printers (Near-quality text and graphics)

If you look at the text printed by a dot-matrix printer, you can see that the characters are all made up by a bunch of dots—hence the clever name. Each of these dots is made by a small rod (a *pin*) pressing the ribbon to the paper.

Checklist

✔ Dot-matrix printers are popular printers for two reasons: they're cheap (you can get one for less than $200) and they're sturdy. Dot-matrix printers are good for areas that have dust or other crud lying about; an environment that would choke a more dainty printer doesn't phase dot-matrix printers at all.

✔ Dot-matrix printers are incredibly noisy, sort of like having a lawn mower sitting by your desk. You might want to get a special cover for the printer to mask some of the sound.

✔ The first popular kind of dot-matrix printer has nine pins. These are the oldest and cheapest variety, and they create the crummiest looking print (think of a supermarket receipt). This is called *draft-quality* type, which is an apologetic way of saying, "I know I look a fright, but I wasn't expecting company." This type is hard—yea, verily unpleasant—to read.

✔ 24-pin dot-matrix printers are capable of creating what's called *near–letter quality* type, which means that it's *almost* good enough for a business letter. In other words, it still looks a bit ratty. But these printers are cheap and durable, and they're appealing if all you need is legible type on paper.

Dot-Matrix Graphics

Because a dot-matrix printer prints dots, it can print any image that can be described as a pattern of dots. These images can include alphabet letters of various sizes and designs. They can also include graphics, such as charts and graphs. Okay, so you won't produce stunning charts and graphs by using a dot-matrix printer, but you can at least produce them.

CAUTION

Dot-matrix printers are for simple, inelegant communication. With these printers, the message had better be good, because the medium isn't very impressive.

Text-and-Graphics Printers (Suitable for framing)

The best printers available create images out of tiny dots. It's the same basic idea as a dot-matrix printer, but the dots are much smaller and aren't hammered onto the page. They're coaxed on by various ingenious means.

The typical resolution of these printers is 300 dots per inch (*dpi*), which produces text type comparable in quality to that in a newspaper. Most can print in any size, shape, or form. And then there are the graphics....

Looks Great! Less Filling!

High-resolution printers have practical value in addition to their aesthetic advantages. For instance, at 300 dots per inch, you can print legible type that's only 1/16 inch tall. This might mean that a whole spreadsheet can fit on a single letter-size page. And high-resolution printers use text that takes up less room on the page, so documents printed on high-resolution printers use less paper.

But mainly the pages they print look better, which is a good reflection on you.

BUZZWORDS

RESOLUTION

Graphics printers create images out of dots, just like a TV set or your computer's monitor. The smaller the dots, the better they blend into a smooth image. The number of dots per inch a printer can create is called its resolution.

140

> The higher the resolution, the smoother the images it can create. With graphics printers, you're paying by the dot—the more you want on the page, the more you pay for the printer.

Laser Printers (The people's choice)

Laser printers were the first high-resolution printers available to the "common" people. Laser printers made desktop publishing from the comfort of your own office or home possible. These printers remain the most popular high-resolution printer: they're easy to use and require very little maintenance.

Another good thing about laser printers is that they're becoming better *and* cheaper. You can now find a good laser printer for around $900. If you can scrape the money together, it's well worth the investment. After all, the final result of almost all the work you do on your computer will be on a printed page. And the appearance of that page counts to your readers.

Mysteries of Laser Printing Revealed

Inside a laser printer is a rotating drum covered in magical chemicals; the surface of this drum can be electrically charged. A laser beam draws the image of your page onto this drum—wherever the laser beam strikes, it changes the electrical charge on the surface of the drum. The electrically charged areas of the drum attract a fine powdered ink called *toner*. This toner is pressed off the drum (called a *toner drum*) onto a piece of

paper and melted into place. It sounds like voodoo, but it works. (Photo-copiers use the same technology.)

✔ Hewlett-Packard makes the most popular laser printers. This point can be important, since you want your printer to be compatible with your software and *all* software works with Hewlett-Packard printers (the preceding was an unsolicited plug). The LaserJet III is probably the most popular printer of all time, but it has been re-placed by the LaserJet 4, which is even more powerful, giving an amazing 600 dots per inch.

✔ Most laser printers print at 300 dots per inch (dpi), which is plenty for text and simple graphics. If you need to print high-quality pho-tographs or do typesetting, you'll probably just want to go to a professional typesetter.

✔ Laser printers use toner cartridges, similar to what photocopier machines use. When a cartridge wears out, don't throw it away. Exchange it for a refilled cartridge; toner cartridges are refillable. This little trick saves you money and makes you feel good about contributing less to your local landfill.

✔ Most laser printers make a continuous humming, even when they're not printing—that's just the fan keeping things cool. The sound doesn't bother most people. The actual printing sound is audible, but not annoying—a soft whistle, a few clicks, a whir.

✔ Laser printers need memory too. I know, I know, it's seems like *everything* about computers wants more memory. Well, printers need memory for two reasons: to store the image of the page as it's being assembled, and to store the fonts used to print the pages (learn about fonts in "Giving Your Printer a Font Lift," later in

this chapter). The more fonts you want to use on your pages, the more memory you need. For most people, 1 to 2 megabytes ought to do it. If you're getting a PostScript printer, make sure that you have at least 2 megabytes (see the next section, "Laser Lingo," for the scoop on PostScript printers).

✔ Printers often have plug-in sockets for adding cartridges that expand the capabilities of the printer. You can plug a PostScript cartridge into a printer, for example, and suddenly you've got a much more powerful printer. You also can plug in font cartridges to give your printer extra typefaces. (Learn more about fonts later in this chapter.)

Laser Lingo

Different laser printers talk different "languages." You need to make sure that you buy a printer that uses a language your software understands. The easiest way to make sure that your prospective printer and software can talk the same language is to ask a computer salesperson, "Will that printer work with this software?"

A quick rundown of the main laser printer languages

▼ *PCL 4 and PCL 5:* These languages were created by Hewlett-Packard, but many other laser printers use them too. PCL 5 is the newer and better language—better because it lets you specify any size of print for your text, from almost impossibly small to incredibly huge. Almost all software supports this printer language.

▼ *PostScript:* This is the printer language of choice for Macintosh users, but it has become popular with PC users as well. Until PCL 5 along, PostScript printers were really the only

continues

any-size-of-text-you-want game in town. Now, with other choices available, PostScript's main advantage is that it has a humongous variety of available typefaces. (A *typeface* is a certain way text looks; for instance, the titles and text of this book are in different typefaces.) Its main disadvantage? PostScript printers are more expensive than other kinds of printers.

▼ *TrueType:* If you own Windows, TrueType is the printer language of choice, because it comes free with Windows. With TrueType, you can get any text size on *any* printer—not just laser printers. If you decide you want to use TrueType, you don't have to worry about what kind of language your printer uses, because TrueType accommodates all of them.

LED and LCS Printers

There are other printers that work very much like laser printers, but without the laser. These are *LED printers* and *LCS printers*.

An LED is a *light-emitting diode*, which is basically an eensy-teensy light bulb. LEDs can be arranged in a grid—300 to the inch—and used to charge a toner drum just like a laser.

LCS printers use *liquid-crystal shutters*, little windows that can be opened to let light through or closed to remain opaque. These shutters are arranged in a grid, like the LEDs, and when one of them gets the signal, it opens and lets light pass through to charge the toner drum in a tiny 1/300 inch spot.

To look at the page, you can't tell LED type from LCS type from laser type. LED and LCS printers are priced about the same as laser printers, too.

EXPERTS ONLY

Looking under the hood

In terms of computer printers, the *engine* is the part of the machine that moves and marks the paper. The electronics (the brains of the outfit) define which marks go where. The engine of a laser printer is usually manufactured by someone other than the company that sticks its name on the outside, so you'll often hear salespeople boast about the engine of the printer as well as the printer as a whole. As with more and more car engines, most printer engines are made in Japan.

Inkjet Printers

If you think laser printers are some kind of black magic, wait until you hear about the *inkjet*—a printer that spray-paints your pages at 300-dots-per-inch resolutions. Believe it.

An inkjet printer uses a tiny nozzle (or, in a color printer, several nozzles) to spit ink onto the page in a very tightly controlled dot. The results are often indistinguishable from those of a laser, LCS, or LED printer.

Checklist

✔ Most inkjet printers use a disposable printing element that contains a small reservoir of ink and a nozzle to spray the ink onto the page.

✔ Inkjet printers are typically much slower than laser printers. (I'm tempted to make a wisecrack here about the speed of light versus the speed of spit.) But inkjet printers are much cheaper, too—the cheapest way, in fact, to get 300-dot-per-inch pages. If you're not in a hurry, they're a great deal.

continues

I HATE BUYING A COMPUTER!

✔ Inkjet printers are incredibly quiet—virtually noiseless. It's almost eerie.

✔ A couple of annoyances about inkjets: The ink bottles aren't very big, so you'll have to replace them fairly often. If you print large graphics on regular copy paper, the page gets ink-soaked, warped, and takes awhile to dry.

✔ *Bubble-jet printers* are a close cousin to inkjets—they're worth checking out.

Color Printers

There are a number of ways to get color onto the page.

▼ Color dot-matrix printers simply use colored ribbons, and a color 24-pin dot-matrix printer is the cheapest way to create a color page. And it looks it.

▼ You can buy color toner cartridges for laser and laser-like printers (LED and LCS printers), but to print color effectively, you need a laser printer that contains two toner cartridges. (The alternative is to print one color and then switch toner cartridges to print the pages again with the second color.) For the capability to print in only two colors, these printers are overpriced.

▼ Color inkjet (and bubble-jet) printers produce reasonable color quality for presentation graphics, such as graphs, charts, and business documents. They print on plain paper and are the most economical way to produce nice-looking color pages.

▼ Color *thermal transfer printers* (also called *wax transfer printers*) use a special ribbon, but they print with heat rather than impact,

melting the color off the ribbon and onto the paper. Some thermal transfer printers require special paper.

▼ *Dye sublimation printers* are the most expensive color printers. They're used by professional graphic artists because they closely approximate the colors created by professional printing presses. You're better off using the money to make a down payment on a new house.

CAUTION

Most color printers—especially affordable ones—don't do a good job with photographic images; gradations of color tend to look speckled. They're also much more expensive on a cost-per-page basis than black-and-white printers. Color printers work best with illustrations and business graphics.

Giving Your Printer a Font Lift

Back in the old days, when the IBM Selectric typewriter reigned supreme, the part of the machine that actually struck the page was a little metal ball covered with letters and numbers. If you wanted your documents to have a different look, you could remove one ball and stick in a different one. The different balls had the same letters on them, but the letters looked different.

That's the idea behind computer *fonts*. You've always got the same letters and numbers available, but you can give those letters and numbers a different look. In other words, a computer font is simply the electronic version of one of those typewriter balls.

With a computer, however, changing the font in your documents is even easier. Here are some different fonts:

Times

Helvetica

Palatino

`Courier`

Most printers come with at least some fonts built into them. These fonts are stored in special chips, and they ensure that you'll be able to print something, even if you never buy another font. All PostScript printers, for instance, come with Times Roman and Helvetica built in, along with a Symbol font that contains miscellaneous math and science symbols and other characters.

Most fonts are sold on diskettes, just like any other software. Once the fonts are loaded into your computer, your programs can use them to print; if you're using Windows and some other programs, you can even see the fonts on-screen.

Some printers also use fonts that come in *cartridges,* in which the fonts are stored permanently in memory chips. Font cartridges are more expensive and increasingly less popular than disk-based fonts.

Printing Speed

The advertised speed of a printer (rated in pages per minute) describes how fast the motor of the printer can pass paper through the printer. In other words, it ignores the amount of time it takes for your computer (or your printer's computer) to figure out how to draw the page in the first

place. A complex page—a page with a lot of fonts or graphics—might require five minutes of computing before printing can begin.

Checklist

✔ When you're printing a number of identical pages, the printer can run at its rated speed. But how soon that first page is ready is anybody's guess.

✔ The real speed of a printer depends on the power of the microprocessor that's building the page images. That microprocessor can be in either the printer or your computer.

✔ How important is the printer's speed? That depends on how many pages you print each day. If you print fewer than 50 pages per day, a 4-page-per-minute printer will be fine. If you need to print more, find a printer that prints 6 or 8 pages per minute.

✔ Remember, you pay for any "extras" with the printer you buy, including speed. You can save money by buying a slower printer and saving large print projects for when you go out to lunch or go home for the day (yes, it's fine to leave the computer and printer on overnight).

CAUTION

A printer is not a printing press, so don't use it to make dozens of copies of the same page. It's cheaper and less harsh on your printer to print only the original and then use a photocopier to make copies.

The Prices of Printers

You can easily spend more on a printer than on your whole computer. That's because moving parts are more expensive than electronics.

In various price ranges, you'll find large numbers of very similar printers from different manufacturers. It's quite possible that under their slightly varying plastic shells, the printers are indeed the same machine. Most printers—especially laser printers—are made by only a handful of manufacturers. Sometimes the company that puts its name on the outside has created some custom electronics to enhance performance. But often the only thing they've done to make their printers unique is to stamp their name on the outside.

If all you need is a nice-looking page, you can find a good 300 dots-per-inch inkjet or bubble-jet printer for very little money, as little as $250. They print at a maximum speed of about 1 page per minute, but if time is no object, you can live with this print speed. Print your long jobs while you're out eating lunch.

The fastest and most reliable all-purpose printers are laser printers. You'll pay a premium for extra durability, faster print speeds, and more processing power. Laser printer costs start at around $900 and go up as high as you can count.

Once you *have* the printer, though, you're still not finished paying. Remember, you've got to buy ink or toner, paper, and cleaning supplies. And all printers require maintenance.

Hidden printer costs

▼ *Dot-matrix:* Hands down, the cheapest way to print. These start at about $200 (for a 9-pin model) and consume only ribbons and

paper. Apart from the purchase cost, the cost of printing is in the neighborhood of five pages per penny.

▼ *Laser printers:* These printers start at about $900. They typically use plug-in toner cartridges that yield a cost per page of about 2 or 3 cents (higher if you print pages with a lot of black on them). In other words, a cartridge that gives you about 5,000 printed text pages costs about $125–150.

▼ *Inkjet printers:* These start at about $500. They're cheaper than laser printers because they're mechanically simpler. The nozzle and ink reservoir are typically combined in a single disposable snap-in unit that prints up to 1,000 text pages and costs in the neighborhood of $25–35, yielding a per-page printing cost similar to laser printers.

Remember this!

▼ There are two basic kinds of printers: Dot-matrix printers do "near-letter quality" text and "near quality" graphics. Graphics printers create smooth, slick type and graphics.

▼ There are several different graphics printer technologies, all of which provide similar high-quality images at 300 dots per inch and up.

▼ A graphics printer uses a special language to create the pages it prints. PostScript, PCL, and TrueType are the leading printer languages.

▼ Each printer language needs fonts specially designed for it.

▼ If all you want is a paper record of the things you've typed and the charts and graphs you've made, a dot-matrix printer is fine. You won't impress anyone with the quality of its pages, but you can definitely get your point across.

continues

Remember this! (continued)

▼ For a slick-looking black-and-white page, the best bargain on the block is a small inkjet printer. Its main liability? It's slooooowwwww.

▼ For high-resolution and faster printing, step up to a laser printer. To save money, get one that doesn't use PostScript and that prints at a modest four pages per minute.

▼ If you're a desktop publisher or graphics artist, go with a PostScript printer.

CHAPTER 13

Cool Toys for Your Computer

(Just in Case You Have Some Money Left Over)

IN A NUTSHELL

▼ Modems
▼ CD-ROM drives
▼ Scanners
▼ Large-screen monitors

W hen you buy a car, the additional goodies you can add to it are called *options*. On a computer, they're called *peripherals*. Some are much more peripheral than others. This chapter gives you a rundown on the most popular ones, in terms of usefulness, price, and hidden costs.

Modems
(The telephone connection)

A *modem* is a gizmo that lets computers talk to each other over telephone lines. The word *modem* is an abbreviation for modulator/demodulator, which I know you're thrilled to hear.

EXPERTS ONLY

You say tomato, I say 100010111000101001

Your computer speaks digital—that is, its language consists of a stream of 1's and 0's. But your telephone transmits analog signals—in other words, sound waves. A modem translates between the two, turning digital to analog, so your computer can send information out over the lines, and from analog to digital, so it can understand incoming calls from other computers.

Things to do with a modem

▼ Send electronic mail to other computer users. Services such as MCI Mail, CompuServe, and Prodigy, for instance, use a huge computer network that works like an electronic post office. By making a local call through a modem, you can use your computer to drop (or receive) a file—text, graphics, or both—to anyone else who has a mailbox. It's a marvelous service.

▼ Dial into computerized bulletin boards, where an entire information flea market has grown up over the past few years. Through these bulletin boards, you can:

> Discover hordes of free, public-domain software placed there for your benefit by generous companies and individuals.

> Contact various and sundry groups who use the service for electronic town-hall meetings.

> Find "user groups" who use the same computers and programs as you, and who can help you with technical problems.

> Drain your entire bank account by paying your monthly phone bill after you've become an on-line info junkie.

▼ Or you can simply dial up someone else's computer directly to exchange files. This method is often the easiest way to exchange files between PCs and Macintoshes.

Modem Speeds

Modems are getting faster, but they're still pretty slow. The phone company loves them. The current standard speed (also called *baud rate*, if you like talking tech) for a modem these days is 2400 bits per second (bps), which means that you can send the equivalent of about four double-spaced typewritten pages of text per minute. Modems that can send up to 9600 or even 14,400 bits per second are becoming more common, though. Since these newer, faster modems can also send and receive at the old 2400 standard, they're worth considering. Check out the next "Experts Only" box for more details.

CHAPTER 13

When you're going to use your modem, consider whether it's worth the time. Graphics files, which are much larger than text files, can take a long time—an hour or more—to send via modem. If you have to send a graphic file long distance, it might be cheaper and easier to call an overnight courier service.

BUZZWORDS

BAUD RATE

Where do they get these words, anyway? The baud rate of a modem is the speed with which it can pass information. If it can pass 1200 bits per second, its baud rate is 1200. Technically speaking, stating the baud rate is not exactly the same as simply saying "bits per second." But un-technically speaking, it's close enough.

EXPERTS ONLY

Should I buy the fastest modem I can?

You can buy modems that can transmit at 9600 bps or 19,200 bps, but there are no industry-wide standards for working at these speeds. If you want to work that fast, your best bet is to make sure that the computer you're communicating with is using the same make and model of modem as you are.

Someday all phone lines will be fiber-optic cables, which transmit your phone calls using light, not electricity. When that happens, modems won't be necessary anymore because fiber-optic wires can handle the digital signals that computers produce. The speed of such communications will be blindingly fast. And the money you save by not needing a modem can go toward buying an expensive digital telephone.

Internal vs. External Modems

You can get an *internal modem*, which fits into an expansion slot inside your computer, or you can get an *external modem*, a self-contained one that sits by itself on your desktop.

Internal modems are cheaper (as little as $69) because there's less to them. There's no housing, for example, and no blinking lights.

If you want blinking lights (so you can watch as the bits go whizzing past), get an external model, which has the added advantage of working with any personal computer. They start at about $150.

"I HATE THIS!"

You mean I have to buy ANOTHER @$%#&*! program?

You need a special program to use a modem—a telecommunications program. These programs work with any modem, but they don't usually come with the modems. You have to pay extra for them. But if you use Microsoft Windows, you get one for free. It's not a very good one, but at the price, who's complaining?

Fax Modems

A *fax* (short for *facsimile*) is like a photocopy you can send over the phone lines. Normally you make a fax by feeding a printed page into a fax machine, which creates a 200-dots-per-inch replica of the page. This "page" gets sent across the phone line and reassembled by a fax machine at the other end.

A *fax modem* shortcuts the process by creating a fax directly from your computer so that you don't have to print the page first. Likewise, a fax

modem also can receive a fax transmission from another fax machine, which it stores in electronic format. You can view the faxes you receive on-screen, or you can print them out.

TIP

For those in quest of the mythical paperless office, fax modems are very nice things, but they're better for the sender than the recipient. If you want to receive faxes, you have to have your computer turned on all day. If you're on one coast and receive cross-country faxes, your computer has to be on three hours longer than your normal workday. More and more often, people are using sophisticated fax machines that can be programmed to send faxes unattended in the middle of the night, to take advantage of cheaper phone rates. But if you want to get those midnight messages, you'll have to leave your computer on 24 hours a day.

CD-ROM Drives

CDs (compact discs) for computers are becoming a popular way to publish information. To use one with your computer, you need a CD-ROM disk drive, which is more expensive than the kind you play music with.

You can buy the entire works of Shakespeare on a CD, or you can get reference materials, such as dictionaries, encyclopedias, thesauruses, and so forth. Some application programs are now available on CD as well.

BUZZWORDS

CD

A computer CD (compact disc) is basically the same as a stereo CD. In fact, a computer CD player can play stereo CDs, allowing you to hear Beethoven over the three-inch speaker in your personal computer.

But since they're for computers, we couldn't just call them CDs, could we? Instead, we have to call them "CD-ROMs." That's ROM, as in "read-only memory," as in your computer can read these disks, but you can't record on them.

Checklist

▼ CDs can hold an enormous amount of information—in the neighborhood of 700 megabytes. In theory, they're like SuperTurboMegaFloppyDisks, except they're not floppy.

▼ Another advantage of computer CDs is that they don't wear out. The information on them is permanent and can't be erased.

▼ One *disadvantage* of computer CDs is that you can't put *new* information on them. This means you can't copy your own files and programs onto the CDs. They're only good for the programs that come on them.

▼ CDs are slower than your hard disk, so don't expect things to happen quite as quickly as if you were running a program from your hard drive.

TIP

> CD drives represent a technology that's still waiting to become really useful. Unless you have a specific need for one right now, put off buying one for a year or so until some standards are established for erasable CDs—that is, when you can play *and* record on them.

Scanners

A *scanner* makes electronic versions of printed images. It's like a photocopying machine that gives you an image on a floppy disk instead of on paper. They're very slick.

Scanners are most commonly used for creating electronic versions of photographs and line art (such as an architectural drawing) that can be incorporated in pages by using a desktop publishing program.

Types of scanners

▼ The most popular scanners are called *flat-bed scanners*, and these do indeed look a lot like a photocopier. You put your original image face down on the glass "bed," and it's scanned from beneath, just as with a photocopier. This process makes flat-bed scanners good for scanning images that are in books and other bound publications.

▼ Cheaper are *sheet-fed scanners*, which have a typewriter like carriage through which you feed the page you want to scan. Sheet-fed scanners are mechanically simple, but they're no good for scanning images from books, for example, or images that are on anything thicker than a sheet of paper.

▼ And then there are small *hand-held scanners* that can capture only a narrow swath of the page as you slide it along. If you want the

whole page captured, special software can stitch the various swaths together into a cohesive whole. Quite slick and very economical, the hand-held scanner is the cheapest of all scanners.

▼ You also can get a *slide scanner*, whose specialty is scanning 35mm slides.

▼ But wait there's more—you also can use a device called a *frame grabber* to capture images from a video tape. This gizmo sits between your computer and your VCR, displaying the video image-by-image on your computer screen. When you find one you want, you can copy it onto a disk. This is a good way to capture 3-D images that a normal scanner cannot.

▼ A similar technology is the *electronic camera* (or digital camera), which instead of using traditional film, captures images on a tiny floppy disk.

How a Scanner Works

Scanning is like laser printing run in reverse. Instead of deciding what a dot should look like and laying it down on paper, a scanner divides the page into a grid and looks at each square (or pixel) to decide what its nature is. If it's a black-and-white image, the scanner judges how light or dark each pixel is. If it's a color image, it also judges what color each pixel is.

EXPERTS ONLY

Impressive-yet-useless information on CCDs

Here's an acronym to impress your friends and awe your adversaries: *CCD*, which stands for *charge-coupled device*. In simple-to-understand Star Trek terms, a CCD is a sensor.

continues

continued

Scanners and electronic cameras use teeny CCDs laid out in a grid, and each one senses the lightness or darkness of one pixel's worth of the image being scanned.

The lightness value of each pixel is converted into a number—digitized—to create a numerical representation of the image that the computer can use to re-create the captured image. Magic.

How Scanners Compare

The points of comparison among scanners have mostly to do with how the scanner captures information and how much detail it can record.

▼ The first variable is resolution—how small the dots are that it looks at, and how finely the scanner subdivides the page. As with a printer, the higher the resolution of the scanner, the more faithfully it can reproduce an image.

▼ The second variable is how much information the scanner records about the nature of each pixel. If it uses 8 bits of information to describe each pixel, a scanner can distinguish 256 distinct values for each pixel. That could be 256 colors or, if it's a black-and-white scanner, 256 levels of gray.

▼ A good color scanner will dedicate 8 bits of information to each of three colors—red, green, and blue—that make up each pixel. That's 24 bits per pixel. A scanner like this can create an image that looks as good as one in a slick color magazine.

The Hidden Cost of a Scanner

The more detail the scanner can record, the bigger the files it can create. A high-quality desktop scan of an 8-by-10-inch color photograph (24 bits per pixel at 300 dots-per-inch scanning resolution) can be over 20 megabytes in size.

Moral: If you buy a scanner, you'd better have a very large hard disk to go along with it, at least 200 megabytes. Not to mention some way to save your scanned images permanently. A high-quality scan will not fit on a floppy disk.

TIP

You also can use a scanner for totally non-pictorial purposes. You can buy programs—called *optical character recognition* (OCR) software—that can decipher scanned text and convert it into electronic text files.

This capability is great for converting typewritten or printed pages, such as newspaper clippings, into files you can use on your computer. In other words, you don't have to retype the text. If you have an old book or manuscript that you'd like to edit on your computer, OCR software and a scanner can turn it into a text file you can attack with your word processor.

You should note, though, that no OCR software is perfect. The computer won't be able to recognize all of the characters, so make sure that you proofread everything you scan.

Large-Screen Monitors

An oversized monitor is luxurious, but expensive. For graphic arts professionals, they're a must. A large screen—say, 19 inches from corner to opposite corner—is big enough to see two facing magazine pages side-by-side at full size. It's also big enough to see a large photograph on-screen.

Checklist

▼ Oversized monitors also give you enough screen acreage to see your work and to have room for all the on-screen "toolboxes" and menus that graphics programs often display.

▼ Professional word processors will appreciate having a vertically oriented full-page screen that shows a full business letter page at life size.

▼ It's not unusual to spend $2,000 or more on a large monitor. They are definitely big-ticket luxury items.

▼ Apart from their size (and price), large-screen monitors are just like any other monitor.

CHAPTER 14

Programs and the Computers They Need

(The Love Connection)

IN A NUTSHELL

- ▼ High-end and low-end programs
- ▼ Word processing
- ▼ Spreadsheets
- ▼ Databases
- ▼ Graphics, business, and professional
- ▼ Educational programs
- ▼ Desktop publishing
- ▼ Games

I HATE BUYING A COMPUTER!

I n the world of computing, having the right tool for the job means owning the right application program and a computer that runs it well. But different applications place varying demands on your computer. Some are simple enough to run on just about any computer that has a keyboard and a monitor; others will take all the computer power you can throw at them and still scream for more.

In this chapter, you'll go through the major categories of software to see what each of them requires in the way of computer hardware. Your mission: to buy a computer with all the features you need, without paying for bells and whistles you won't use.

TIP

ATTENTION, PC SHOPPERS! Don't assume that you need Microsoft Windows! DOS programs have their advantages; for instance, they run faster than Windows programs, mainly because the computer spends much less of its energy on the operating system. Windows might offer a lot of slick services, but it's a lumbering hulk compared to DOS. The bottom line: you can get good performance from a DOS word processor with a much less powerful machine than it would take to run the Windows version of the same program.

Professionals and the Rest of Us

In every software category is a range of products from the high end (high quality, lots of capability, and a hefty price tag) to the low end (simple or entry-level programs with a modest ticket price). To run well, high-end products always demand a more powerful computer than low-end ones. And every good salesperson will try to convince you that you need the professional model.

But often what distinguishes a high-end program from a low-end one is a lot of capabilities you don't need. For example, if you're looking for a word processor so that you can type letters to Aunt Wilma, you may not need any high-end bells and whistles such as:

▼ Automatic footnoting

▼ Automatic indexing

▼ The capability to include graphics on your pages

▼ The capability to create multicolumn pages like you see in magazines

Because program manufacturers compete on the basis of how many features their programs contain, it's hard to buy one that does only what you need. But in any case, don't be put off by the label "low end." If you buy a high-end program and use only it's low-end features, you've wasted your money.

CAUTION

All the hardware requirements prescribed in this chapter assume that you're buying a new computer (the pros and cons of buying a used computer are discussed in Chapter 14). In fact, some of the "minimum requirements" listed here are in fact overkill for the applications cited. But I've done this for two good reasons: to assure the resale value of your computer, and to ensure against the increased demands of tomorrow's application programs. In other words, you might not outgrow your computer, but the rest of the world might.

TIP

Many computers are sold with a choice of several major application programs thrown in for free (well, they don't charge separately for them, and the price is much lower than you could otherwise get). These are generally high-end word processors or spreadsheets, or an "integrated software package" such as Microsoft Works that includes a low-end word processor, spreadsheet, and database all in one package. Because these programs normally sell for several hundred dollars each, this package deal is a very economical way to buy your principal application program.

Word Processing

Word processing is a horrible term. I don't like to think of my words as being processed any more than I like to think of my food being processed. But I guess that's just my tough luck.

Word processing is probably the easiest task a computer is typically asked to perform. In other words, you can "word process" with any personal computer. Word processing affects the kind of computer you buy when you start getting fussy about how the words look on your screen and how they look on the printed page. Fussiness is next to costliness.

On the Macintosh and on PCs running Microsoft Windows, a word processor can show you the words you type in their proper size, in their proper typeface, and with their proper spacing, indents, and line endings. The only difference between the page you see on-screen and the page you print is that the type on the printed page will be crisper and smoother, printer willing. Working this way can save time and effort

because you never see any surprises when the page is finally printed—the mistakes are visible on-screen.

But on the PC, you have the option of a simpler, less accurate screen display. All you need is a word processing program that operates under DOS. Most PC word processors are available in both DOS and Windows versions.

TIP

DOS word processors are the choice of many professional word processors because they're faster than graphical programs and they don't rely on using a mouse. Good typists can work much faster when they keep their hands on the keyboard and off the mouse. And professionals don't need such an easy-to-use interface, because through hours of constant use, they know their program coming and going and don't need the friendly reminders offered by the Mac and Windows interfaces. How can you type fast when your program is always holding your hand?

Whatcha Need?

Application programs typically advertise minimum system requirements to let you know what kind of computer you need to run the program. But these aren't always (or even often) the requirements to run the program *well*. (It's sort of like saying you can carry 10 people in your Volkswagen Beetle—you can, but it's not very comfortable.) To assure good performance, look for an application program's recommended configuration, which tells you how much computer you need to use the program effectively.

I HATE BUYING A COMPUTER!

Word processors: Minimum hardware requirements

▼ Black-and-white monitor (VGA for PCs)

▼ Memory: 2 megabytes for DOS word processors, 4 megabytes for Windows and Macintosh word processors

▼ Microprocessor: 80386 (PC), 68020 (Macintosh)

▼ Hard disk: 80 megabytes

Word processors: A possibly useful option

▼ For the PC, a mouse (all Macs come with a mouse)

Spreadsheets

Spreadsheets, like word processors, don't demand much oomph from your computer. You don't need a color monitor, and you don't need the most powerful microprocessor. Of course the more complex your spreadsheets, the more powerful you'll want your computer to be. Basically, though, number crunching (the high-tech way to say "working with spreadsheets") calls for a no-frills computer.

But what you *do* want is a nice screen display that can clearly show legible numbers in fairly small sizes. Although it's nice to see numbers that are large and easy on the eyes, it's also useful when working with a spreadsheet to have the option to see as many rows and columns on-screen at one time as possible. The smaller the numbers your program can display, the more numbers you can fit on-screen. Such displays are available in the leading (and more expensive) DOS spreadsheets, so you don't need Windows.

When a Picture Is Worth a Thousand Numbers

Major spreadsheet programs do more than just crunch numbers laid out in grids; they also can create graphs and charts based on those numbers. (There's nothing like a nice colorful pie chart to make impending bankruptcy look more palatable.) If you plan to create charts and graphs, you'll want a color monitor and probably a color printer as well. This will add at least $1,000 to the cost of an otherwise simple accountant's system.

But again, on the PC side of the fence, color graphing and charting is included in high-end DOS spreadsheets, so you still might not need Windows.

Spreadsheets and Coprocessors (Faster, Faster, Faster)

The major spreadsheet programs can all take advantage of a *math coprocessor chip* to speed up their work. But unless the spreadsheets you create are very large, very complicated, or linked to other spreadsheets (you can create overlapping spreadsheets in which changes in one affect the numbers in others), you might not benefit greatly from a math coprocessor. Math coprocessors are fairly expensive—about $200—so don't rush out and buy one unless your program's manufacturer actually recommends that you use one.

BUZZWORDS

MATH COPROCESSOR

A computer chip you can add to your system (if it doesn't already have one) to speed up the rate at which your computer system performs math computations. You'll especially notice the change in speed if you use a spreadsheet program or any other program that performs gobs of calculations.

I HATE BUYING A COMPUTER!

Spreadsheets: Minimum hardware requirements

▼ Black-and-white monitor (VGA for PCs)

▼ Memory: 2 megabytes for DOS spreadsheets, 4 megabytes for Windows and Macintosh spreadsheets

▼ Microprocessor: 80386 (PC), 68020 (Macintosh)

▼ Hard disk: 80 megabytes

Spreadsheets: Possibly useful options

▼ Color monitor for creating graphs and charts

▼ Math coprocessor

TIP

Some microprocessors come with built-in math coprocessors. This setup is true of the 80486DX (PC) and the 68040 (Macintosh). It may not be much more expensive to buy a machine with one of these chips built in than it is to add a math coprocessor to a lesser machine.

Databases

Databases are super librarian programs. Their job is to store huge amounts of information (which calls for big hard disks) and to retrieve that information in any form you can imagine. A company might use a

database, for example, to keep track of all their suppliers and customers, keeping track of their addresses, their purchases, their credit histories, and so forth. When you call the phone company and they ask you for your phone number, they use that as an I.D. number to look you up in their database.

TIP

Database work is one job for which you should definitely shop for the software first, and then buy a computer to match its needs. Database programs can be very complex and power-hungry, and the demands they place on a computer vary a lot.

Database work is all computation and very little display, unless the data you're filing is graphical, such as the photographs used by a real estate agency or the illustrations used for a manufacturer's parts catalog.

CAUTION

You can't just unpack a database program and begin using it. You've got to configure it so that it does what you need—pretty high-level computer programming stuff. You might need help from a computer nerd to assemble your database before you can begin putting your information into it.

Pros Prefer PCs

The best, most powerful, and most popular database programs run best or exclusively on PCs, and most of those run under DOS. PCs running DOS can devote more of the computer's processing power to the database, and databases want all the power they can get. Although there are excellent middle-range and low-end database programs for both Macs and PCs running Windows, both of these machines spend too much

energy on the operating system to run databases as fast and effectively as the pros want.

Databases: Minimum hardware requirements

▼ Black-and-white monitor (VGA for PCs)

▼ Memory: 4 megabytes for DOS databases, 8 megabytes for Windows and Macintosh databases

▼ Microprocessor: 80386 (PC), 68030 (Macintosh)

▼ Hard disk: 80 megabytes

Databases: Possibly useful options

▼ 256-color monitor (for photographic databases)

▼ 68040 (Mac) or 80486 (PC) microprocessor

▼ A larger hard disk

▼ A second hard disk for constant backup

Finishing Tools

Database programs are good for storing, sorting, and retrieving information, but they're typically not very good at creating handsome presentations. If your database reports have to be good-looking (if, say, you're in real estate and want to generate a list of potential properties for a client), you'll probably want a good word processor or desktop publishing program to create jazzy finished pages.

CHAPTER 14

Graphics

There are two basic kinds of graphics: business graphics (such as charts, graphs, and slides for presentations) and graphic arts graphics (including illustrations, artwork, and photo retouching). The main difference between the two is that business graphics are typically printed on the desktop and duplicated on a photocopier, whereas graphic arts graphics are printed on high-quality professional printing presses.

Both require color computer systems, but graphics arts computers need more of everything: memory, colors, speed, and hard disk storage.

Business Graphics Programs

Most business graphics are created for in-house documents and presentations, such as sales reports. Such pages can be printed well by using a high-resolution color printer, such as a color inkjet printer. The idea of business graphics is to communicate effectively, not necessarily to cause people to swoon over the artistry of your presentation.

Also known as *presentation graphics* programs, the applications used to create these graphics can also be used to make color 35mm slides directly from your computer files.

Business graphics programs: Minimum hardware requirements

▼ 16-color monitor (VGA for PCs)

▼ Memory: 2 megabytes for DOS business graphics programs, 4 megabytes for Windows and Macintosh business graphics programs

▼ Microprocessor: 80386 (PC), 68020 (Macintosh)

▼ Hard disk: 80 megabytes

I HATE BUYING A COMPUTER!

Business graphics programs: A possibly useful option

▼ 256-color monitor (for more color choice, smoother color blends)

Graphics Arts Programs

Traditionally, graphic arts professionals have preferred Macintoshes, but with the latest version of Microsoft Windows, more and more high-end graphic arts programs are migrating to the PC, and the graphic artists are following suit. For graphic arts programs, DOS is not an option; it doesn't support color or graphics well enough.

Graphic arts programs are among the most technically complex you can use on a desktop computer, and some—such as photo retouching programs—require as much power as you can throw at them. They suck up as much money as you can throw at them, too.

Graphic arts programs: Minimum hardware requirements

▼ 256-color monitor (VGA for PCs)

▼ Memory: 8 megabytes

▼ Microprocessor: 80386 (PC), 68030 (Macintosh)

▼ Hard disk: 120 megabytes

Graphic arts programs: Possibly useful options

▼ Double-page (19-inch) monitor

▼ 16.7 million–color monitor (24-bit color)

▼ More memory (16 to 32 megabytes)

▼ 80486 (PC) or 68040 (Mac) microprocessor

▼ Math and graphics coprocessors

▼ 200+ megabyte hard disk

▼ Cartridge drive for storing large files (see Chapter 11)

Educational

Some children's programs are overtly educational; some, like illustrated books on disks and CDs, combine entertainment with education. Because these programs are interactive—your kids make decisions about what the program does—kids don't just sit passively as they do in front of a TV. They get involved with the computer.

Educational programs are meant to run on computers that schools can afford, that is, inexpensive computers. Programs that use a mouse are easier for kids to handle, so if you're shopping for a PC, look for a model that includes one, even if you don't use Windows. Color will certainly make using the computer more appealing for kids.

BUZZWORDS

INTERACTIVE

When you use an interactive computer program, there's a give and take between you and the program. It asks you questions, you give it answers, and vice versa. A child's interactive book-on-a-disk, for example, lets a kid determine the plot of the story or even take the place of one of the characters. So

continues

continued

when your kid and Floppsy the Bunny come to a fork in the road, your child can decide whether they go left or right. Or if Floppsy becomes boring, your kid can invite other characters into the plot, and the story changes accordingly. The story need never be the same twice.

Educational programs: Minimum hardware requirements

▼ 16-color monitor (VGA for PCs)

▼ Memory: 2 megabytes for DOS programs, 4 megabytes for Windows and Macintosh programs

▼ Microprocessor: 80386 (PC), 68020 (Macintosh)

▼ Hard disk: 80 megabytes

▼ Mouse

Educational programs: A possibly useful option

▼ CD drive (see Chapter 11 for details)

Desktop Publishing

Desktop publishing is by far the most demanding of all desktop computing applications. It combines high-end word processing, professional graphics, and complex page-assembly software that can make pages as

slick and complicated as any you'll see at the magazine stand (in fact, many of the ones you'll see there have been created with personal computers).

There's a wide range of programs for desktop publishing (or *DTP,* for the acronym-starved), and they include programs for making everything from Sunday-school announcements to million-dollar glossy magazines. For that reason, I'll outline two sample systems here: one for low-end work (including newsletters, flyers, invitations, in-house presentations—laser-printed stuff, by and large) and one for high-end, professional documents (such as color "coffee table" books, magazines, and annual reports).

Desktop publishing: Minimum low-end hardware requirements

▼ 256-color monitor (VGA for PCs)

▼ Memory: 2 megabytes for DOS programs, 4 megabytes for Windows and Macintosh programs

▼ Microprocessor: 80386 (PC), 68020 (Macintosh)

▼ Hard disk: 80 megabytes

Desktop publishing: Minimum high-end hardware requirements

▼ 16.7 million-color double-page monitor (19 inches, 24-bit color)

▼ Memory: 8 megabytes for Windows and Macintosh programs (there are no high-end DOS DTP programs)

▼ Microprocessor: 80486 (PC), 68040 (Macintosh)

Destktop publishing (continued)

▼ Hard disk: 200+ megabytes

▼ Math and graphics coprocessors

Desktop publishing: Possibly useful options

▼ Cartridge drive for saving large files (see Chapter 11)

▼ Scanner (see Chapter 11)

Games

For good game playing, you want a computer that's fast enough and colorful enough to create a good, smooth screen display for the increasingly slick animation that games use nowadays. You'll also want a soundproof room so that the rest of the family isn't tortured by the various clunks, booms, screeches, and laser blasts whining from your computer's speaker.

Games: Minimum hardware requirements

▼ 16-color monitor (VGA for PCs)

▼ Memory: 2 megabytes for DOS games, 4 megabytes for Windows and Macintosh games

▼ Microprocessor: 80386 (PC), 68020 (Macintosh)

▼ Hard disk: 80 megabytes

Games: Possibly useful options

▼ 256-color monitor

▼ For PCs, an extra serial port (or two) for a game controller such as a joystick

BUZZWORDS

JOYSTICK

A joystick is an alternative to the mouse that's built expressly for playing computer games. It consists of a vertically mounted handle that moves from side to side and to and fro—actions that steer the cursor around the screen. Buttons on the handle can shoot down aliens, return backhand tennis volleys, steer a Formula-1 race car, or outdraw Black Bart at the O.K. Corral.

PART III

Taking the Plunge

Includes:

CHAPTER 15

Obsolescence
(The Mighty Dread)

IN A NUTSHELL

▼ Obsolescence defined
▼ Out-of-date or just out-of-style?
▼ Prices and obsolescence
▼ Your best defense

Obsolescence is the ultimate paranoid bugbear for the computer buyer. How can you be sure that the slick machine you buy today won't be just a quaint conversation piece by next year?

This chapter shows you how you can deal with the threat of obsolescence.

What Does It Mean To Be Obsolete?

The computer industry pumps up the fear of obsolescence to sell new computers. The fact is that no computer is obsolete as long as it does the job you need it to do. Out of date, yes, but obsolete, never. With computer technology advancing at its current rate, *every* machine you get will be out of date within months. This fact doesn't matter because the computer's still just as useful as the day you bought it. Don't get trapped into the "keeping up with the Joneses" computer-buying syndrome. You'll go broke that way.

You can still use an out-of-date computer, but you can't use it for as many things as a new computer. At worst, you're stuck in the not-too-distant past. The following sections deal with some concerns you may have about your computer becoming obsolete.

Old Programs, Old Capabilities

If you have an out-of-date computer, you have to use older versions of programs because newer ones demand more memory, speed, or disk storage than your computer can provide. A PC from 1983, for example, can still process words like a pro, but word processing programs from 1983 can't use a laser printer.

Old Operating Systems, Old Programs

Older computers can't run newer operating systems. Without an 80386 PC, for instance, you can't profitably run the current version of Microsoft Windows. Most new programs require the latest operating system, so an old operating system freezes you in the past. Is that bad? Not if the computer you're using does what it needs to do, it isn't.

Old Computers, Small Resale Value

Older computers are hard to re-sell. Fewer and fewer people want to use yesterday's programs, and with the declining prices of new and more powerful personal computers, you may have a hard time selling an old machine even at a garage sale.

You won't ever be able to justify the cost of any computer if you think of it in terms of resale value. You may not be able to get more than a fifth your original purchase price if you try to sell your computer. In the time you own the computer, though, you should save in time and effort, many times more than the cost of the machine. In that light, a computer is a very good investment.

What Makes a Computer Out-of-Date?

The pacesetter of technical progress is the microprocessor manufacturer. Each new generation of microprocessor creates capabilities that are taken advantage of by newer generations of operating systems.

On the PC, the march of progress in chip design has defined when a computer is out of date. The 80286 of 1985 closed the door on the 8088 and 8086, for example, and the 80386 of 1988 closed the door on the

I HATE BUYING A COMPUTER!

80286. With prices on 486 computers coming down, it may not be too long before the last 386 rolls off the line. And there's *always* something newer and faster in the works.

On the Mac, a combination of chips and other hardware have made older models passé. The original Macs couldn't accommodate enough memory to run later operating systems. Old 512-kilobyte and 1-megabyte Macs can't run many of today's programs.

The vicious cycle of computer evolution

▼ The more a new microprocessor can offer, the more a new operating system can do.

▼ The more the new operating system can do, the bigger it gets.

▼ The bigger the operating system gets, the more memory it needs.

▼ The more memory the computer uses, the less is left over for application programs.

▼ The more memory the programs need, the more you have to buy for your computer.

▼ The more memory computers have, the more complex the applications become.

▼ The more complex the applications become, the more they need a more powerful microprocessor.

But Hey, It's Today . . .

If you buy a computer that's immediately surpassed by tomorrow's model, the absolute worst thing that can happen is that you're locked into doing on it what you can do today. If you know exactly what you want to do, and you're happy doing it the way you're doing it, that's fine. No sweat, no threat.

. . . And Yesterday's Not That Long Ago

There are so many old computers out there (they don't die; they don't even fade away) that there's still an enormous amount of software available that can run on ten-year old personal computers. Replacement parts are still available for all but the most obscure brands of PCs (although they may cost more than the computer's worth). In other words, most software vendors aren't dumb enough to turn their backs on the over 100 million personal computers now in use, even if many of them are out of date. Your computer will never be orphaned by a cruel and insensitive computer industry.

"I HATE THIS!"

Do I really need the fastest, most powerful, and fanciest computer?

The truth is that today's personal computers are much more powerful than most people need them to be. This fact means you're paying for more machine than you need, but it also means that your purchase isn't likely to go out of date very fast. Of course, software and hardware manufacturers have an abiding interest in selling you newer, better toys, so it's always in their best interest to make you feel that your equipment is woefully out of date.

Price and Obsolescence

No major purchase you can make—with the exception of a truckload of fresh fish—will lose its value faster than a computer. Just by virtue of its being used, it diminishes in value, just like a second-hand car. On top of that, the prices of computers are coming down all the time. These facts suggest two buying strategies, which are covered in the following sections.

Savings Come to Those Who Wait

Don't be the first one on your block to buy a computer that uses the latest microprocessor. Within a year of their introduction, new generations of computers traditionally sell for a fraction of their original asking price. When 80386 PCs first came out, they sold for $3,000. Today, you can get one that runs twice as fast as the originals for less than $1,000. 80486 machines are following the same pattern.

Look for a Short Payback

Don't buy a computer with the hope of selling it later to get your money back. Your machine has to pay you back by being an able assistant, not by being an investment or a source of lasting equity.

Defenses Against Obsolescence

Traditional wisdom among computer veterans is, "Buy all the power you can afford." There's some truth to this old chestnut. But the more practical path is buy all the *potential* power you can afford. In other words, buy a machine that can be expanded if your needs change.

Checklist

✔ You want a computer that can be expanded up to at least 16 mega-bytes of memory even if you think 4 megabytes is already insane.

✔ If you're looking at an 80486-equipped PC, remember that the 80486DX chip can have its clock speed doubled (see Chapter 5) at some later date by buying a special adapter chip.

✔ PCs that use 80286 chips are already out of date, although they're still being sold. They can only be used efficiently with DOS, not Windows. Don't buy a 286 computer unless you don't care at all about obsolescence.

✔ Macintoshes with 68020 chips are falling behind the pack. Some graphics programs are beginning to specify a 68030 chip as the minimum needed to operate them.

✔ Buying a too-powerful computer is ultimately a less costly mistake than buying one that's not powerful enough. In truth, the prices aren't all that different. (For the trappings of power, see Chapter 5.)

✔ The successor to Microsoft Windows—called Windows NT —is apt to take up over 40 megabytes of hard disk space all by itself. You may not need Windows NT (it's really intended for networked business computing environments), but it's an indication of the kind of megabyte-munching software that's coming down the line. SuperMegaHog operating systems will come to the Macintosh as well, probably in the form of System 8.

THIS BEEPING PILE OF PLASTIC JUST AIN'T A TYPEWRITER.

WHERE'S THE DING?

IN THE GOOD OLD DAYS OF NEWSPAPERING YOUR TRUSTY TYPEWRITER WOULD HELP YOU EXPRESS YOURSELF...

YOU COULD POUND THE KEYS HARDER WHEN YOU WERE MAD...

AND PLAY THAT UNDERWOOD LIKE A PIANO WHEN YOU FELT POETIC.

MOST IMPORTANT, THOUGH, WAS THE WAY YOU COULD BLOW OFF STEAM WHEN YOU MADE A MISTAKE...

TAPPA... TAPPA... TAPPA... PATTA....

YOU COULD RIP OUT THE PAPER, CRUMPLE IT UP AND HEAVE IT ACROSS THE NEWSROOM.

ZIP!

SOMEHOW IT MADE YOU FEEL A LOT BETTER WHEN YOU DID THAT...

BUT TODAY, WITH THESE WORD PROCESSORS AND COMPUTERS,.... WELL, IT JUST AIN'T THE SAME...

BUT IT'S STILL PRETTY SATISFYING.

CHAPTER 16

Where To Buy It

IN A NUTSHELL

▼ How retail channels vary
▼ Computer stores
▼ Computer superstores
▼ Consumer electronics stores
▼ Department stores
▼ Custom-made computers
▼ Mail order
▼ Second-hand computers

I HATE BUYING A COMPUTER!

The first time I saw a ComputerLand store selling retail computers in a California mall I thought, "These guys are nuts, this'll never catch on." (I also thought Reagan was unelectable.) But now you can buy computers in department stores, next to the lamps and chairs. You can call an 800 number, rattle off your credit card number, and have a spanking new computer delivered to your doorstep the next day. Computers are for sale everywhere.

You can buy a computer in lots of ways and places, and this chapter takes a look at the pros and cons of each of them. They differ in a lot more ways than just the prices they offer.

How retail channels vary

▼ **Price:** You can get good computer prices just about anywhere, but you can find some of the best deals through mail order and in the superstores—those warehouse-sized buildings with stuff stacked to the ceiling.

▼ **Range of selection:** Obviously, smaller places are going to have less of a selection on hand, although they can probably order it if they don't have it in.

▼ **Ability to dispense useful advice and information:** This is one of the most elusive parts of computer buying. When you find a good computer salesperson, latch on to him and never let go. Ask friends for recommendations or go to a local computer user group and ask them for advice on good places to shop.

▼ **Ability to offer hands-on test drives:** Unfortunately, you can't test drive equipment you're buying through mail-order. To compensate for this problem, most mail-order houses have no-risk guarantees.

▼ **Service after the sale:** Some places have on-site service; some even send the repairman to you so that you don't have to lug the computer to them.

▼ **Availability of training programs:** Will they help you learn how to use the incredibly sophisticated piece of equipment they just sold you?

▼ **Warranty protection:** All warranties are not created equal. Make sure they'll service what they sell, and that you don't have to pay for it.

Computer Stores

A computer store is the most logical place to shop for a computer; after all, they sell nothing but computers. The people who work in computer stores are fairly knowledgeable, but often only about the specific models of computers they sell. They're there to help you make up your mind, so pick their brains.

Many computer stores are authorized dealers for particular brands of computers. This status means that you can get manufacturer-authorized repairs and services there. It's also additional evidence that they know what they're talking about.

Pros

▼ Expert advice available

▼ After-sale service at the store

▼ Training available

▼ Test drives available

Cons

▼ Limited selection

▼ Extra services mean somewhat higher prices

Computer Superstores

These stores are high-tech versions of the consumer warehouse stores where you can buy crates of toilet paper and canned peas by the ton. Their emphasis is on volume sales, which means low prices, a wide selection, and usually scant service or scantily informed salespeople. You may find more forklift drivers in these stores than computer experts.

Depending on the selection available, you may want to shop at such a place if you already know just which computer you're after.

Pros

▼ Low prices

▼ Wide selection

▼ One-stop shopping for all your computer needs

Cons

▼ Less experienced salespeople

▼ Little (if any) training and after-sales support

▼ Limited or no repair service

Department Stores

The only reason to buy a computer at a department store is that you may find an amazing deal there. To department stores, computers are no different from wheelbarrows or washing machines—if something's not selling, the store often slashes prices just to get the merchandise off the floor.

If you already know what kind of computer you want (and it's not a whiz-bang turbo state-of-the-art machine), check for sales in major department stores before taking the plunge elsewhere.

Pros

▼ You can shop for your computer and your fall wardrobe under the same roof.

▼ You may find a terrific deal.

Cons

▼ No top-of-the-line equipment

▼ Lack of expert salespeople

▼ Lack of after-sales support

▼ No training services

▼ No service department

Mail Order

Mail-order companies can offer the lowest prices for PCs and Macintoshes because these companies are low-overhead outfits: no fancy showrooms, no salespeople. (And occasionally, no scruples.)

To keep costs down, more and more PC-compatible manufacturers only sell direct to consumers by mail order. Some mail-order companies simply resell computers built by other companies, but if you're going to buy through mail order, you're better off buying direct from the manufacturer.

Shopping in the Dark

The problem with mail-order PCs is that you're buying blind. Before buying, try to get a demonstration of the machine somewhere—at a computer show (your best bet), at a store, or on the desktop of a satisfied customer. Most of these mail-order machines are rated by PC magazines from time to time, although their tests are cursory and provide little insight into the health of the company (you want it to outlive your warranty, at least).

You can also buy a Macintosh through mail order (in which case you know just what you're getting), but the prices aren't that much lower than in stores. You also need an authorized Apple dealer in your area in case your Mac needs repairs.

CAUTION

All it takes to be a mail-order computer company is a magazine ad and a telephone. Some of these companies come and go alarmingly fast, so do a little research before you buy. Computer magazines rate the major mail-order companies

(both Mac and PC) from time to time, so check recent issues in the library for the latest survey. A call to the Better Business Bureau doesn't hurt either.

Pros

▼ The lowest prices

▼ The widest selection (there are hundreds of mail-order companies)

Cons

▼ Service centers are usually nowhere near you. This is not a problem if the company offers on-site service. On-site service means that if something goes wrong, the company takes care of sending a repair-person to you.

▼ Difficult to arrange test drives

▼ Hard to gauge the company's reputation. There are a few tried-and-true mail-order companies you can trust, however, including Dell, Zeos, Gateway, and Compaq. These companies are every bit as trustworthy and likely to be around as your local computer store.

TIP

When buying a mail-order computer, make sure you get a very good warranty. If your machine needs repairs, you'll probably have to send the ailing part to a service center far, far away. If this situation occurs, make sure you don't have to pay for shipping in either direction.

Custom-Made Computers

There are many small companies that will build a PC for you on demand. Sometimes they advertise in computer magazines, but often you'll only find them by combing the Yellow Pages.

These companies use industry-standard parts and can whip up a computer that meets your needs within a week or so. Their prices are low because they have very little marketing overhead and no inventory to speak of.

Some of these companies are very small indeed—virtual garage operations. To protect yourself, find out how long they've been in business, and get a list of previous customers you can call.

Pros

▼ Offer computers made to your specifications

▼ Low prices

▼ Service and repairs near you

▼ Expert advice by the people who actually assemble the computers

Cons

▼ Small companies with limited track records could be here today and gone tomorrow, which leaves you with no service or warranty.

▼ No test drives

▼ No training

Used Equipment
(Do you feel lucky?)

Buying a used computer is like buying a used car, and people are of two minds on this subject:

Sage Advisor A: "When you buy a used computer, you're just buying somebody else's problems."

Sage Advisor B: "Computers are tough; I don't need new equipment, and the resale prices are so low that this is a deal I can't pass up."

Which brings us to the question: Do you feel lucky?

TIP

You can do most computing tasks, with the exceptions of desktop publishing and fancy graphic arts work, on almost any computer. But before you buy an older computer, make sure the programs you want to use will run on it. Or better yet, try to find an older computer that's being sold with programs of the type you want to use.

Used computer considerations

▼ A computer doesn't have a mileage meter. You have no way of knowing how much it's been used or abused.

▼ Computer warranties are typically non-transferable (although there's nothing to keep you from claiming to be the original owner). Read the warranty well, in any case.

continues

I HATE BUYING A COMPUTER!

Used computer considerations (continued)

▼ Because the market for used computers is soft, you should get a very good deal. Even on a nearly-new computer (whatever that means—demand to see a dated sales slip), don't pay more than 75% of the price of an equivalent new machine.

▼ You should be able to get a very low price on an out-of-date machine such as PC-AT (with an 80286 microprocessor) or a Macintosh Plus (with its 68000 chip). See Chapter 13 for insights on obsolete equipment.

TIP

Computer shows are great places to do some comparison shopping. In addition, manufacturers often have show specials, which enable you to cart off a computer at a special discount. Sometimes, in the waning hours of such shows, exhibitors will sell off their display models so they don't have to lug them home. You may have to pay $25 to get into one of these shows, but, when you compare it to the cost of a new computer, it's not a bad investment. Spring and fall are the big computer expo seasons.

CHAPTER 17

Warranties
(No Strings Attached—Or Else!)

IN A NUTSHELL

▼ Duration of coverage
▼ Who handles warranty obligations
▼ Where repairs take place
▼ The ideal warranty defined
▼ Lemon protection
▼ Service contract pros and cons

I HATE BUYING A COMPUTER!

ood news: personal computers don't break down very much. But that doesn't mean warranties aren't important—you still need protection against defective parts and shoddy workmanship. And not all warranties are the same, not even close.

This chapter chops through the thicket of small print and explains the different kinds of warranties now being offered on personal computers.

Time Is of the Essence

Typically, personal computer warranties last for one year, with the cost of both replacement parts and labor covered for the duration. Longer is better, of course, but shorter is unacceptable.

In addition, many computer sellers—particularly mail-order houses—offer 30-day money-back guarantees in case you change your mind for some reason about the computer you've bought. You might discover that the machine was misrepresented to you, that it won't run the programs you'd hoped, or that your "I hate buying a computer" attitude has shifted smoothly into a hatred of *using* the &*!!$# thing, too. In any case, within the first 30 days, irreconcilable differences should be grounds for an uncontested divorce from your computer.

Who's Responsible, and Where Are the Repairs Made?

You want all of your warranty problems to be handled by one source, one that's close to you and your computer.

But there are three different agents who could wind up servicing your warranty:

▼ The people from whom you bought it.

▼ The people who made it.

▼ A separate service company working under contract.

No matter which of these three (or which combination) winds up carrying out the warranted repairs, *you* shouldn't ever have to deal with more than one of them. Because your deal was with the people you bought the computer from, they should be the ones on the hook for fulfilling warranty obligations. You call them; they handle the rest.

Features of the ideal warranty

▼ Your dealer handles the warranty; you address all warranty problems to them.

▼ 2-year (or more) warranty on parts and labor.

▼ 30-day, no-questions-asked, money-back guarantee.

▼ 90-day immediate free parts replacement.

▼ All parts warranted by your dealer, not just the manufacturer.

▼ Fast, free, on-site repairs for all parts under warranty.

▼ All defective parts replaced, not repaired.

▼ Free 24-hour hotline for service questions for the duration of your warranty.

continues

I HATE BUYING A COMPUTER!

Features of the ideal warranty (continued)

▼ Free loaner replacement equipment for the duration of the repair.

(This is not a fantasy list—warranties like this actually exist. You want one. It's worth paying a few dollars extra for.)

Warranty Service from Your Dealer (Your best choice)

If you buy your computer from a dealer near you, your best bet is to get them to carry your warranty, for several reasons:

▼ They're close by, so you can easily bring in parts that need service.

▼ They know you, your work, and your machine.

▼ They can't give you a hard time because you'll spread the word that they're creeps.

Warranty Service from the Manufacturer

Getting your computer serviced by the manufacturer can also be an excellent option, but only if the manufacturer has authorized dealers in your area who will promptly carry out warranted repairs.

If the manufacturer has no local authorized repair shops, someone is going to have to pay for shipping your sick machine to some remote computer clinic. Under the terms of many warranties, you're on the hook for shipping costs, which can easily exceed repair costs. A free repair shouldn't cost you any money, right?

Warranty Service from a Contractor

To serve their customers better, many computer dealers and manufacturers contract out warranty repairs and service to other companies who specialize in the field. Some of these service agencies are quite large, run by companies such as General Electric. Often these service companies provide on-site service—that is, they come to your computer and fix it right on your desktop.

For mail-order companies, using a service agency is a very common way to provide warranty service. But if your local computer store wants to pawn off warranty service to such an organization, resist. To the computer store, you're a customer (presumably a valued one), but to the service agency, you're just a faceless name on a list. If possible, you want to deal with someone you have some leverage over: the people from whom you bought your computer.

CAUTION

On-site service sounds like a great idea, but it's not so great if you have to wait for a week or two for a repairperson to show up at your door. When you're thinking about buying a computer that has an on-site repair warranty, ask specifically how long it will take a repairperson to come to your address. If you can get fast on-site service, you couldn't ask for better coverage.

Lemon Protection

Some computers were born under a bad sign. Just as you can get stuck with a lemon automobile, you can purchase a lemon computer. A good warranty offers protection against such sour experiences.

CHAPTER 17

Checklist

✔ Look for a warranty that guarantees immediate replacement of parts that croak within 90 days of purchase.

✔ If you receive a lemon component, don't settle for having it repaired. You want a new one.

✔ Don't accept any delays in getting you that replacement. You should be able to waltz into your dealer with the bum part and have it replaced right there and then.

TIP

When it comes to warranties, be tough. The people who guarantee your computer are gambling with your time and work, not just their own profits. If the machine fails, they owe you, and they should pay up immediately. Resist any warranty that puts any responsibility on you to do without prompt replacement parts, to pay for shipping of failed parts (or their replacements), or to suffer any undue inconveniences.

Extended Service Contracts

Sometimes you can pay extra to have your warranty extended or to buy a separate extended service contract. A good warranty doesn't need to be enhanced by a service contract for which you have to pay extra. Service contracts should pick up the slack only when your original warranties have expired.

The wisdom of these options depends on how you feel about buying insurance in general. Companies wouldn't offer these deals if they

weren't going to make money from them, so you might consider self-insuring your computer: put the money aside so it'll be there if you need it.

Things a service contract needs

▼ Coverage of all parts (except ones you negligently ruin by spilling your Fanta on them), not just "defective" parts

▼ On-site or close-to-home repairs

▼ Free loaner equipment if repairs take a long time

▼ No fees or expenses (such as shipping) over and above the cost of the contract

TIP

If you use your computer at home, make sure that your home-owner's insurance policy covers it in case of fire, theft, or accident. Many home policies classify computers—along with works of art—as objects that need to be covered by a special rider, at extra cost. (Note that your home-owner's liability insurance will not protect you from claims by your neighbors that their kids' brains were turned to putty playing computer games at your house.)

PART IV

Up and Running

Includes:

CHAPTER 18

Setting Up
Your New Computer
(The Proud Owner)

IN A NUTSHELL

▼ Taking inventory
▼ Finding a good home for your computer
▼ Loading your software

I HATE BUYING A COMPUTER!

The check has been written; the deed is done. There's a stack of boxes marked FRAGILE sitting next to your desk. Now what?

This chapter is going to walk you through those first tenuous hours to get you up and running successfully with no sweating and no fretting.

Take Inventory and Follow Directions

First, open all the boxes, take everything out of them, and place the contents on your desk. There's always a packing list that tells what you should find in all the boxes. Make sure that you have everything you've paid for.

Don't put any computer part on the floor once it's out of the box; keep everything up above dust level. The machine will suck up its share of dust over time, so at least try to get a clean start.

Among all the parts, you'll find the beginning of a small computer library. Locate the book (or, better yet, a booklet) that's entitled something like "Getting Started" or "Setting Up Your System." Read it from cover to cover and make notes in it about what steps you should take in setting up. It's very unlikely that after setting up your computer great clouds of smoke will billow out of it, but if they do, you want to be able to say, "But I was just following your instructions!"

Do's and Don'ts for setting up your computer

▼ Don't have your computer screen facing a window, or you'll be tormented by its reflection on-screen. Find someplace where ambient light or glare won't affect your view of the monitor.

▼ Don't put your computer under an open window, under an air conditioner, over a heater or heating vent, or in any other place where dusty air regularly flows. In general, you want your computer's new home to be clean. A computer's fan will suck in whatever happens to be drifting past: dust, smoke, soot, and so on. Some PCs have a little air filter over the fan opening, but once this is clogged with dust, air will find its way in some other way.

▼ Do put the computer on a sturdy piece of furniture. For the sake of the hard disk, which is very vulnerable when it's spinning, don't set the computer on a piece of furniture that's likely to get bumped into, is on wheels, or that, if jostled, will sway or bump against the wall.

▼ Do keep all the computer's wires up off the floor. You sure don't want anyone tripping over them, and you don't want to have the wires getting nudged loose by a rogue vacuum cleaner.

▼ Do make sure that the cables connecting the CPU to the printer and monitor are securely plugged in. Tighten the screws or fasten the clamps.

▼ Don't ever play with those wires while the power is turned on.

▼ Do feel free to put the monitor on the CPU box; it's sturdy enough to support the monitor. This might coincidentally put the monitor at a comfortable height for you. But maybe not. The center of your screen should be somewhat lower than the tip of your nose when you're seated in front of your monitor. This will have you looking slightly downward at the screen, the most comfortable position for head, neck, and shoulder muscles.

▼ Do locate the air vents of your computer, monitor, and printer, and make sure that nothing's blocking them. The vents are usually on the sides and top of the units. Overheating is a computer's worst enemy.

TIP

When you buy your computer, buy a power strip with a surge protector. A power strip is basically a short extension cord with a bunch of sockets into which you can plug your computer components. The surge protector is a fuse that will protect your equipment against a sudden surge of electrical power coming across the lines, as can happen during an electrical storm. In the unlikely event that a tidal wave of electricity roars down the wires, the $10 power strip will be scorched, but your $1,000 computer will be spared.

CAUTION

If you whack a hard disk drive while it's running, its recording head will likely hit the disk and remove large divots from it. This is called a hard disk *crash* (a very appropriate choice of words, for once). Hard disk crashes are rarely simple fender-benders. Even if your hard disk survives, the information stored there is likely to be lost.

Loading Software

Your computer may have come with software already loaded on the hard disk. If so, you don't have to load (or "install") your software. It's done for you. Hoorah! All you have to do is plug the pieces of the computer into each other and into the wall. Turn it on, and away you go.

If you bought a PC without the software, you'll have to load the operating system software yourself. On the Mac, this process is meticulously outlined in the Mac's getting-started manual. In fact, the information is baby-fed to you in such little spoonfuls that you'll be tempted to start skipping pages. Don't.

Loading DOS and Windows
(The first PC steps)

On the PC, loading DOS is simple—just follow the instructions in the manual. If you're loading Microsoft Windows, first make a list of the specific parts of your computer; the Windows installation program specifically asks you about the following parts:

▼ What kind of mouse you have.

▼ What kind of monitor your have.

▼ What kind of display adapter you're using.

The Windows installation program might ask questions you can't answer or that simply don't make sense. In these cases, Windows will suggest an answer for you, and you can simply accept it. For example, it might ask, "Where on the hard disk do you want the Windows software installed?" A reasonable answer to this question is, "How should I know??!!" But the friendly installation program will suggest a place, a place called "Windows." A fine idea; accept it.

After the operating system software has been loaded, both Mac and PC hardware experiences are just about over, apart from feeding floppy disks into the thing. You'll be spending almost all of your time dealing with software. The only hardware struggle you're likely to have is remembering where the on/off switches are.

Checklist

✔ It's a rare thing for a computer not to have DOS and Windows pre-installed when you buy the computer. Insist on having pre-installed software; you shouldn't have to be the one to go through the drudgery.

continues

I HATE BUYING A COMPUTER!

Checklist (continued)

✔ Currently two common versions of DOS are available: Version 5 and Version 6. Both are good, but Version 6 has some features that make it an irresistible bargain, such as an "undelete" feature that makes it easy to get back files you've accidentally removed, an anti-virus feature to help you guard against computer viruses, and a file-compression utility that lets you get twice as much information onto your hard disk. Ask for DOS 6.

CHAPTER 19

The Care and Feeding of Your New Computer

IN A NUTSHELL

- ▼ Good computer hygiene
- ▼ Healthy disk habits
- ▼ Where to go for help

Y ou bought your computer. You figured out how to make it run. This chapter takes you the next step: How to keep that thing running now that the check has cleared the bank and it's yours, all yours.

Computer Hygiene

Computers are amazingly durable, considering the tiny size of most of their components. Nevertheless, you should adopt good computing hygiene habits to ensure a long, healthy life for your machine.

Keep It Clean

Computers dislike dust and other airborne pollution. Smoking around your computer isn't strictly taboo, but the smoke and flying ash from cigarettes winds up in your floppy disk drives and can gum up the works. Ashes in the keyboard aren't good either. Underneath every key is a little switch that can get clogged up with bits of garbage that slip down between the keys.

The fan that cools your computer also sucks dust, so keep the area around your machine as dust-free as possible. Computer dust covers (a towel is fine—you don't have to pay money for these things) will keep assorted crud from settling out of the air and into your CPU, monitor, and keyboard.

Use a Mouse Pad

A mouse pad is a special little pad with a textured surface that the ball under the mouse can get a good grip on. If you use a mouse directly on

the top of your desk instead of a mouse pad, the ball carries bits of desk sludge up into the works of the mouse, and eventually the mouse stops working correctly—your cursor hesitates, jerks, and misbehaves. You can open up the mouse and clean the accumulated gunk off the little rollers inside it, but it's better not to let it get dirty in the first place.

Keep Magnets Away from Your Computer

Magnets can erase or scramble information stored on a computer disk— hard or floppy—so if you think it would be a cute idea to use your favorite refrigerator magnet to stick memos to your CPU, think again.

Use Only Approved Materials in Your Printer

Laser and laser-like printers use a heated roller to fuse the toner particles onto the page (see Chapter 10 for details). This same technique is used in a photocopying machine, so anything that's specifically approved for use in a photocopier will work fine in your laser printer. These items include self-adhesive labels and clear acetate sheets made for use with overhead projectors.

Don't Leave Your Computer Running All the Time

Turn off your computer if you're going to be away from it for an hour or more. Computers are tough, and it doesn't hurt to leave them running for hours on end, but why should they suffer the extra wear and tear if they don't have to?

There is a cult of computer users who believe that it's actually better to leave their machines on all the time instead of turning them off when

they're not in use. If this is true, computers are the only machines in the world to work this way. I don't believe it for a minute.

Never Change Connections with the Power On

If you want to connect or disconnect a printer cable, modem cable, or another wire, cable, or connection on your computer, always turn the power off first. Computers hate sudden surges or cut-offs of power, so you should change connections only when no electricity is flowing. Besides, you don't want Kentucky-Fried fingers, do you?

Good Disk Habits

Hard disks and diskettes need tender loving care to keep them working their best. Use the techniques described in the following sections.

Keep Your Diskettes Covered

If you use 5 1/4-inch diskettes, always store them in their paper sleeves. Also, buy a dust-free box to store your diskettes in (whichever size diskettes you use). You can buy diskette storage boxes at any computer or office supply store.

Defragment Your Hard Disk

Hard disk fragmentation sounds catastrophic, but it's happening constantly while you use your computer. This term just means that the sectors on the disk have been written over so many times and in so many

patterns that files wind up being recorded in tinier and tinier pieces, spread out farther and farther all over the disk. This break-up of files makes retrieving them much slower, so your whole computer slows down.

Special defragmenting programs tidy up this mess. PC owners get a defragmenting program free with DOS. Mac owners have to buy one separately.

Make Backups of All Important Files

Information on a computer disk is really pretty fragile. The most sane policy is to be completely paranoid about the security of your files and make duplicate copies of everything.

Backup procedures

▼ Back up everything onto floppy disks. Twice. If you make only one backup copy for the archives and that disk croaks (it happens, believe me), you're up bit creek without a paddle.

▼ Don't put all your backups in the same place where they can suffer from the same disaster. Businesses should keep a second set of backup disks at another site in case of fire, theft, or other calamity.

▼ Back up your programs as well as your data files.

▼ Back up your hard disk as often as you can stand to. With a hard disk, you have all your eggs in one basket. If your data is crucial, buy an automatic backup system that will back up all your files at some appointed time of the day (for details, see Chapter 11). With this program, you'll never lose more than a day's work if the hard disk fails.

TIP

When you're working on your computer, everything you do is hovering in the electronic ethers until you save it to a disk. Get into the habit of saving every few minutes. When you pause for a thought, hit the Save button. When the phone rings, hit the Save button. The first time you lose a half-hour's work because of a program crash, a power drop, or someone tripping over the power wire, you'll feel very, very bad. Then you'll remember having read this, and you'll feel even worse.

Where To Go for Help

Computer questions and problems always pop up. Why doesn't the cursor move any more? Why doesn't my document print? Is the monitor supposed to be smoking like that?

You can turn to a number of places for answers. But before you start making phone calls, please note that 90% of the questions that program users ask program manufacturers are answered with: "You'll find that information on page XXX of your program's manual."

In other words, look it up in the manual first. The answer is probably in there somewhere. Keep in mind that most computer problems are software problems. But when that tack fails, start making phone calls in the sequence shown on this list. The first two steps will probably be the only ones you'll have to take.

Places to call when you have computer problems

▼ **The shop where you bought your computer (or application program).** You gave these people a lot of money. They should be happy (or at least willing) to help.

▼ **The manufacturer of the program you're using.** Often, the manufacturer has a toll-free number you can call for answers to technical questions. Be prepared to describe your computer and the other programs you're using. Also be prepared to be put on hold.

▼ **The manufacturer of your computer.** This manufacturer has lots of your money too, and more and more often manufacturers are competing on the basis of their reputation for helpfulness.

▼ **Any computer, software, or computer repair store.** Make some local calls to see whether anyone is familiar with your problem. Don't expect or ask for elaborate free advice. Just get some simple clues.

▼ **A bookstore.** There are billions and billions of computer books out there, one of which may answer your question. Be sure to always, always, always buy from Que. And I'm not just saying that because Que publishes this book.

▼ **Local user groups.** By inquiring in your local computer-selling community, you should be able to track down a local user group, a bunch of computer users who have been drawn together by enthusiasm, despair, or need for mutual support. These folks are great sources of useful information.

▼ **On-line services.** Using a modem to connect your computer to your telephone line (would-be telecommunicators, see Chapter

continues

I HATE BUYING A COMPUTER!

Places to call when you have computer problems (continued)

11), you can tap into electronic bulletin board services (BBSs). These are large information-exchange services, and they usually have special interest groups for specific computing subjects. These electronic user's groups often have question-and-answer bulletin boards for use by folks just like you.

▼ **Computer magazines.** The magazines themselves aren't apt to be right there with an answer, but their editors might be. Find a magazine that looks like it talks about your kind of work, and call up its technical editor. These characters know a lot, and are usually very helpful people. And busy, too. So don't tell them it was me who sent you.

PART V

Quick & Dirty Dozens

I HATE
Quick & Dirty Dozens

IN A NUTSHELL

▼ 12 questions to ask the sales-person

▼ 12 questions the sales-person is likely to ask you

▼ 12 things you should buy to go with your computer

▼ 12 scary computer problems and what to do about them

▼ 12 upgrades to consider (a computer wish list)

▼ 12 fun things you can do with your computer

12 Questions To Ask the Salesperson

1. "How does this model compare to...?"

Try to get specific explanations of why the salesperson claims that one model is better or worse than another. The difference might have little or no bearing on what you want to do with the machine. Or perhaps the extra money you might pay for some swell feature will never pay you any dividends. A 256-color monitor, for example, probably won't make any difference to you if you don't plan to print in color.

2. "Why is that important?"

Just as restaurants make their big money on drinks, computer manufacturers make their big money selling bells and whistles—whiz-bang features you may not need. Because you can't count on computer salespeople to have an objective viewpoint of the relative importance of these features, always steer the conversation back to how a particular feature affects the work you plan to do.

3. "Exactly how much faster does that make it?"

Your computer can never be too fast, but don't pay for speed enhancements you can't use. Very fast computers are great for database work and graphics applications, for example, but they don't make your word processing go much faster. Again, get the salesperson to relate the alleged speed advantages to your specific job.

4. "Do you service these computers right here?"

You want the answer to this one to be yes. If you have a problem with your computer, you want it serviced on the spot, not boxed up and shipped to Timbuktu for repairs.

5. **"Do you own a computer yourself? What kind?"**

Don't try to put the salesperson on the spot, but ask about his or her own computing preferences and experiences. This humanizes the conversation and gives you some clue as to where the person is coming from. If it turns out that she designs anti-ballistic missile guidance software in her spare time, you've learned that her perspective may be a wee bit skewed.

6. **"Which computer do you recommend for my kind of work, and why?"**

Don't forget to ask why. Remember that computer salespeople have to be jacks of all trades, and they might not understand your particular application all that well.

7. **"Do you plan to have a sale in the next 60 days?"**

It doesn't hurt to ask. Most salespeople are pretty honest about this kind of thing, but don't expect them to volunteer the information if you don't specifically ask about it.

8. **"Do you know of any new models coming soon from this manufacturer?"**

Newer might mean both cheaper and better. These days, there's tremendous pressure for all computer manufacturers to keep prices as low as possible, so ask about potential bargains coming down the line.

9. **"How long has this computer manufacturer been around?"**

There are over 40 major manufacturers of personal computers plying their wares in the U.S. today, and there are dozens of minor players. But just because you've never heard of a particular manufacturer doesn't mean that their machines aren't top-notch.

Look for a manufacturer with a proven track record, but don't feel obliged to buy a machine emblazoned with a famous name (for which you'll likely pay extra).

10. **"Which is your most reliable model?"**

In general, personal computers from major manufacturers are quite reliable, but certain models might have a track record of problems and breakdowns. If the salesperson doesn't have the information, ask to speak to the shop's service technicians.

11. **"What software comes with the computer? Will you install it for me?"**

These days, the computer world is a buyer's market. Dealers should be willing to toss in something to sweeten the deal, typically the operating system and an application program or two. Negotiate to have the dealer install your operating system software for you and to install any free software as well.

12. **"What discount will you give me if I buy a printer from you too?"**

It's possible that your best deal on a printer won't be found at the same place where you buy your computer. To make up for this, ask for a discount on the printer. Just say, "But I can get this printer for $100 less at Wild Wally's Computer Barn." If you have technical problems later, it'll be easier for you to get help if you bought your whole system from one source.

12 Questions the Salesperson Is Likely To Ask You

1. **"How much do you have to spend?"**

Dodge this one. You should walk into the store with an idea in your head of how much you want to spend, but it should stay right there. The chances are good that the computer that's right for you will cost less than you think, so there's no point in advertising that you're willing to spend more.

2. **"What do you plan to do with the computer?"**

An excellent question, and one you should try to answer as fully as possible. Even if you don't really understand enough about computers to know what you want to do, describe your work as best you can.

If you want to create documents, bring samples of what you'd like them to look like. If you're buying for a student, bring him or her along—don't try to buy a computer as a surprise present unless you already know about computers and you know what that person wants to do with the computer.

3. **"Do you want Microsoft Windows?"**

If you're buying a PC-compatible computer, you probably do want Windows; it makes learning and using the computer much, much easier. And because most computer dealers throw in Windows for free when you buy the computer, there's no reason to say no. But this is the chance to get an education about how Windows works and what its advantages are.

4. **"Do you have a particular program in mind?"**

You may have seen an application program that seems just perfect for you, but stay open-minded. If you think you know what you want, say so, but also ask to see programs that the salesperson thinks are competitive with it.

Also keep in mind that certain programs make specific demands on the computer they run on, and the program you want might require a computer that's too expensive.

5. **"Are you familiar with Windows (or the Macintosh, or anything else)?"**

This is an invitation for an education you can't turn down, so always say, "Oh, just a little." If a salesperson is eager to teach you things, always go along. If the lesson is going too slowly, you can step up the pace, but never turn down a free tutorial.

6. **"What kinds of pages do you need to print?"**

Another excellent question. For many applications, especially desktop publishing, the look of the printed page defines the system and the software you need. For others, such as word processing, there are many systems that can create a very similar-looking page. Whenever possible, bring samples, and don't just say something like, "Oh, you know, business letters and stuff."

7. **"Is color important to you?"**

"Yes, I'd like a blue one," is *not* the correct answer. When thinking about color computers, start at the printed page. If you don't plan to print in color, you don't need elaborate color on-screen. 16 colors is plenty for most applications if you don't plan to print in color. An exception is games, where lots of colors (say, 256) on-screen make things much more fun.

8. **"Do you need to exchange files with another computer?"**

If the answer is yes, specify the kind of computer. You'll want a computer with floppy disk drives the same size as the machine with which you'll be communicating.

9. **"Do you expect to connect this computer to a network?"**

This is a variation of the previous question, but the ramifications are more far-reaching. If you'll be connecting your computer to a network, you might need special cables, add-in boards, and software to make the connection possible. Your dealer should install all of these things for you.

10. **"How much memory and disk storage do you want?"**

You should have a rough idea of what you need, but if you can get more for a bargain price, go for it. With software becoming hungrier and hungrier for memory, it's becoming harder and harder to have too much of it. And because large-capacity hard disks are a relative bargain, computer manufacturers are building in larger and larger ones for very little extra money. A fairly normal amount of memory to want is 4 megabytes; a medium-sized hard drive is about 80 megabytes.

11. **"Do you want to buy some programs to go with it?"**

Answer: "What'll you give me?" The chances are good that you'll find a dealer who will give you for free the principal program you'll be using, especially if it's a spreadsheet or word processor.

It's often cheaper to buy software from a mail-order company than a computer store, so make sure that you're getting a good deal.

12. **"Who told you to ask all these questions?"**

Tell 'em you've got a friend in the business.

12 Things You Should Buy to Go with Your Computer

1. A power strip

A power strip is a block that contains a bunch of electrical outlets and a surge protector, which is a fancy name for a fuse. You plug the power strip into the wall and all your computer parts into the power strip. Then if there's a sudden surge of power over the electrical lines—like during a thunderstorm or your neighbor's kid's science fair experiments—the $19.95 power strip will get fried instead of your computer.

Since most computer mishaps involve damage from power surges, a good power strip is the best investment you can make in your computer's health.

2. A mouse pad

As you slide your computer's mouse around your desktop, it slowly picks up the thin film of gunk that's accumulated there and transfers it into the mouse's innards. No matter how clean you keep your desk, it will develop desk gunk—it's no reflection on you or your housekeeping habits.

A mouse pad has a textured surface that resists desk gunk and is easy to clean. When your mouse is clean, it will work more smoothly...and so will you.

3. A comfortable chair

You'll be spending a lot of time in front of your computer, and you don't want to spend it sitting on an old kitchen chair. You want a chair whose height is adjustable so that your arms are at a comfortable typing height and angle. Your chair should also provide

excellent back support, which will take a lot of strain off your neck and shoulders as well.

4. A fax modem

A modem is a nice thing, and for not much more money, you can buy one that sends and receives faxes as well. This means that you'll never have to print out pages just to fax them, and you can receive any fax as an electronic file, again without paper (printing them is optional).

5. High-quality diskettes

Cheap diskettes are no bargain. It's like buying pants with holes in the pockets. The first time a cheap diskette dies on you and takes all of your files with it, you'll wish you'd spent the extra 50 cents on a good diskette.

6. A dust-proof diskette holder

Diskettes are very vulnerable to dust, cookie crumbs, coffee spills, and other environmental hazards. Treat diskettes the way you treat your eyeballs: keep them protected and dust free, and keep your fingers out of them. Any dust-proof container will do, but you can buy special diskette filing boxes at any stationery or computer supply store.

7. A can of compressed air

Photographers use these for blowing the dust off their lenses, and you can use them for blowing the dust and paper fuzzdies (the "technical" term I just made up for paper lint) out of the guts of your printer. Theoretically, you can also just take a deep breath and blow really hard, but the insides of printers are scientifically designed in wind tunnels to assure that this maneuver will drive all dust directly back into your eyes.

8. A bag of twist ties

No matter how simple you think your computer is, you'll wind up with a spaghetti jungle of wires cascading from its back. Binding them up with twist ties keeps them off the floor, where they're liable to get kicked, yanked, and nibbled on by pets and hungry children.

9. A back-up program

There's no excuse for losing computer data. It's easy to make a copy of everything you create. A back-up program makes it even easier; all you need is the discipline to use it.

You simply tell the program to make a copy of every data file on your computer, which it does on a series of diskettes. Thereafter, you can tell the program, "Make a copy of every file that I worked on today." The program will dutifully copy those files onto the diskettes, cueing you to supply the diskettes it needs. Cheap, painless insurance against losing the files you've worked so hard to create.

10. An anti-virus program

A computer *virus* is a program that copies itself from one computer to another. Your computer can get one by using someone else's diskettes or even by connecting to another computer via phone lines.

Usually viruses aren't meant to be destructive, they're just some techno-vandal's idea of a good time—like painting electronic graffiti inside as many computers as possible. But their creations might interfere with the orderly operation of your computer, and might even destroy your files or programs.

An anti-virus program detects viruses as they try to copy themselves into your computer. They can also eliminate viruses from disks that have already been "infected." Some of the best anti-virus programs are free, so ask around before you spend any money for one.

11. A printer cable

As unbelievable as it may seem, printers often come without the cable needed to connect them to a computer. When you're buying a printer, try to get the vendor to throw in the cable for free.

12. A scanner

Scanners are still pretty expensive—perhaps as much as your computer—but if you've got the right job for them, they can be a dream come true. Scanners make digital images of printed pages. If you're in the real estate business, for example, you can use a scanner to create a photographic database. You also use a scanner to convert printed pages into editable computer text, using optical character recognition (OCR) software. If you have a long manuscript to convert from typewritten to electronic form, the scanner might pay for itself in a single job by eliminating the need to re-type the text.

12 Scary Computer Problems and What To Do about Them

1. **The manual doesn't make any sense!**

Don't worry; this is par for the course. Computer hardware manuals are notoriously badly written, and many software manuals aren't much better. In general, read the manuals only to learn specific information. If the manual's answer is unintelligible, get on the phone and call your computer dealer and ask for a translation.

2. **Nothing happens when I turn on the computer.**

It's time to wiggle all the wires. Then take a look at the power strip (if you're using one) to make sure that the switch is turned on there. If it's still no go, bypass the power strip and plug your computer directly into the wall. If there's still nothing, call your dealer and start screaming.

3. **My screen is telling me, "Non-system disk or disk error."**

This message means that the computer can't find the operating system. The most likely reason is that you started the computer with a diskette in a floppy disk drive. PCs always first look for the operating system on drive A. If it finds a disk but no operating system, it throws up its hands and sends an error message. Solution: remove the diskette and tell the computer to try again.

If there's no diskette in either disk drive, you probably have to reinstall (or perhaps install for the first time) the operating system, DOS. This process is pretty easy, and it's adequately described in your computer manual. If DOS hasn't been loaded, Windows probably hasn't been loaded either (if you have Windows), and you'll have to do that too.

4. **My Macintosh is frowning at me!**

During start-up, if you see a sad Macintosh icon instead of the usual happy one, your computer can't find the operating system. First, restart the computer—sometimes Macs have a hard time waking up and need a second chance. If you still get the bad news icon, you'll have to (re)install the operating system, a simple process painstakingly outlined in the Mac manual.

5. **The screen is frozen!**

Sometimes your computer will suddenly freeze up—typing does nothing, the mouse pointer doesn't move, everything seems frozen. Sometimes it just happens; chalk it up to the evil little gremlins that live inside computers.

Whenever your screen freezes, make some notes about what you were doing when it happened: what programs you were using, what command you had just issued, and so forth. If it happens often, something might be wrong with your computer, with the way it's configured, or with the way your programs are interacting. Your notes can lead to a proper diagnosis and cure. In the meantime, just stop swearing, take a deep breath, and restart your computer.

6. **I suddenly got a message telling me to restart my computer!**

This is related to problem number 5, but this time the operating system has been clever enough to spot the problem. There's still nothing you can do about it, though, except to follow orders.

Again, make notes on what you were doing when the error occurred, and write down the error message you received, including any error number displayed. These numbers are almost always meaningless, but occasionally they reveal to a technician what the problem is.

7. **I can't save my work!**

On the PC, you'll get a message saying, "Write Protect Error." On the Mac you'll see the warning, "You cannot copy because the disk is locked." Yes, disks can be locked, but they can be unlocked, too. On 3 1/2-inch disks, you'll find a little sliding door in one corner. If the door is open (you can see through it), the disk is locked; your computer can read from it, but can't record anything on it. On 5 1/4-inch disks, a little square notch is cut out near one corner. If this notch is taped over, the disk is locked, or "write-protected" in PC jargon.

8. **Nothing prints!**

Hoo boy. This is a problem with a zillion-and-one possible causes. Most of the time, though, it's one of four things:

▼ The printer isn't turned on.

▼ The printer isn't on-line, which means that the light beside the on-line button isn't glowing.

▼ The cable to the printer has squirmed loose.

▼ The wrong printer driver or connection has been selected.

Check the first three things first. Then make sure that your programs knows which printer you have and how it's connected to the computer.

9. **My disk is unreadable?**

This could mean three things:

▼ You're trying to use a Mac disk in a PC, or vice versa.

▼ You're trying to use an unformatted disk. Formatting files is easy, especially from Windows; just follow the manual. If you're using DOS, look in your DOS manual for specific examples of how to issue formatting commands.

▼ Your diskette has gone to the great diskette heaven in the sky, taking all your files with it. If you know that your diskette has files on it, try five or six more times to read the disk. Sometimes persistence pays off. If the computer does manage to read the disk, immediately copy all the files to another diskette or to your hard disk. Then reformat the troubled disk. If the computer tells you the formatting has failed, throw the diskette away—it's a goner.

10. Waddaya mean, "Illegal filename"?!

File names can be only 11 characters long: 8 characters, followed by a period (which doesn't count as one of the 11), followed by 3 more characters. Often, application programs use these last three characters—called the *file name extension*—to identify files they've created. This leaves you with just 8 characters for a file name. Using additional characters is a no-no, as is using certain characters, such as spaces, colons, periods (except before the file name extension), commas, or backslashes (\ ).

On the Macintosh, file names can be up to 32 characters long, and the only taboo character is the colon.

11. My work has disappeared!

This happens all the time to users of the Macintosh and Windows. The problem is that you accidentally clicked the mouse outside of the window for your application program. To the computer, this is a signal that you want to switch to whatever it was you clicked in, which is generally the program running in the background.

In Windows, to get back to where you belong, use the "Switch To" command by clicking on the button in the top left corner of the window you're in. On the Mac, if you have System 6, choose the program you want from the Apple menu in the top left corner of the screen. If you have System 7, choose the program from the application menu in the top right corner.

12. **Hmmm...now, where'd I put that file?**

Both the Mac and the PC let you search for files by their names or part of their names (if you can't remember the exact file name). The process is trickiest when you're using DOS. You have to use the DIR command (for listing the contents of a directory) in the directory you think contains the file. The command DIR *.TXT, for example, will list all the files with the file name extension .TXT (the asterisk is a wild-card character that stands for any combination of characters). Likewise, DIR F*.* will list all of the files starting with the letter *F*. Yeah, a very clumsy process.

Searching for files is considerably easier under Windows; use the Search command from the Program Manager's File menu. This command lets you search through an entire drive, not just directory by directory.

12 Upgrades To Consider
(A computer wish list)

1. **A larger monitor**

Scrolling around the page is one of computing's biggest time-wasters. A screen that lets you see a whole page at its true size will save you a lot of time. Graphic artists will appreciate a double-page screen, which allows them to see two facing pages simultaneously at 100%. Besides, a big monitor makes you look like you're a NASA scientist, only cooler.

2. **More colors**

You can see more colors on your computer screen by upgrading its display adapter, the controller card that's mounted inside the CPU. Many display adapters can display more colors if you add more video memory to the board, which you usually can do without having to buy a new monitor. Then you can see those great color photos in real-life technicolor. Whether that's worth the money you'll spend is up to you.

3. **Graphics tablet**

A *graphics tablet* is a kind of electronic drawing pad that lets you use a stylus instead of a mouse to issue program commands and create art works. Because the stylus feels just like a pen, you can do freehand drawings, create a digital version of your signature (to use with a fax modem, for instance), and create many artistic effects.

Special pressure-sensitive graphics tablets enable you to draw thicker lines on-screen by pressing harder on the tablet with the stylus, giving you paintbrush-like control over your artwork.

4. More memory

Computer memory is cheap and getting cheaper, and most computers can accept much more memory than they come equipped with. Adding memory is the easiest way to put more pep into your computer.

5. Additional storage

Hard disks fill up surprisingly fast, so you might want to add another hard disk to your computer. You should have your dealer do this job. An easier (and less expensive) strategy is getting disk-compression software, which tricks the hard drive into thinking that it's bigger than it really is. DOS 6 comes with Doublespace, a disk-compression package, at no extra charge.

6. CD ROM drive

More and more software is being sold on CDs, especially educational and multimedia programs, including dictionaries and encyclopedias.

Anymore, CD-ROM drives aren't too expensive; you'll probably be able to get one for $200–300. (Okay, that's still a lot of money, but you should've seen how much they cost a couple of years ago!) When you do buy a CD-ROM drive, though, you'll save time and anguish by having a professional install it.

7. Envelope feeder

Most printers are notoriously bad at printing envelopes, but by adding an envelope feeder, you can have both plain paper and envelopes ready to print at all times. All you have to do is tell your application which bin to draw its paper from during printing. Make sure that the envelope feeder you buy is designed specifically for the printer you have.

8. A network

Businesses should consider networking when workgroups have to
share a lot of information. Networks wire computers together so
that they can share printers and information. They can be very
simple or very elaborate, but sharing peripherals such as printers
and modems can save a lot of money. Also, having everyone working from a shared electronic filing cabinet can save a lot of time
and confusion.

9. **More printer memory**

If you use a lot of typefaces in your documents, adding memory to
your printer might speed up printing considerably. During printing,
many programs send fonts into the memory of the printer, where
they're used in building the image of the page.

When printer memory is limited, the fonts have to be shuttled in
and out, a repetitive copying process that wastes a lot of time. If
there's enough memory in the printer for all of a document's fonts,
they are downloaded only once, and your pages pop out that much
faster.

10. **Operating system upgrades**

From time to time, the manufacturer of your computer's operating
system will release a new, updated version. The new version will
have a new number. DOS 6, for example, has many improvements
over DOS 5.

When you buy an operating system, be sure to send in your regis-
tration card. That way, you'll be notified when new versions are
available. You'll also get piles of junk mail from software companies
that purchase mailing lists from operating system companies.

11. A modem

Modems let you hook up your computer to your phone line. You can then communicate with other people who use computers on things called *electronic bulletin boards* and *electronic information services*. At first glance, that might sound about as exciting as watching fungus grow—who wants to hang around with computer-lovers? Remember, though, that normal people like yourself now buy computers, and you almost certainly have a lot in common with some of them. For instance, CompuServe, a popular information service, has areas for people to discuss cooking, automobiles, gardening, fiction, movies, and just about everything else you can imagine.

12. A sound card

If you use your computer to play games, a sound card can give it a whole new dimension. With a sound card and speakers, your computer will be able to blast out incredibly life-like sounds and dazzling sound effects.

12 Fun Things You Can Do with Your Computer

1. Do your taxes.

Well, I guess this doesn't qualify as a fun thing, but a computer can take the sting out of the process (and maybe save you some money). Income tax preparation programs are updated every year, and they'll walk you through the whole process so that you don't miss a single deduction. They can print out all the necessary forms in a format acceptable to the IRS. And the cost of the software is tax deductible.

2. Work from home.

It's amazing how much you can get done when you don't have to go to meetings. With a modem, you can stay in constant touch, if you want to. It works for me.

3. Edit videos.

You can connect a VCR directly to your computer (with the proper adapter board) and edit your videos on-screen, copying them back onto another video cassette. Astound your friends with your cinematographic talent, and watch them smile when they realize that they only have to sit through the *edited* version of your trip to Lake George.

4. Catch up on your letter writing...with one letter.

No one has to know that the letter you've written is a form letter. Just add a little personal paragraph to each person you write, and no one will be the wiser. Just be sure that you don't address the envelope to "Occupant."

5. Order pizza.

Now that most pizzerias accept fax orders, you can use your fax modem to order that extra large heartburn special and tack a map on the bottom to expedite its delivery to your door.

6. Address your Christmas card envelopes.

Nobody would wish you a case of writer's cramp for Christmas, so next year, use your computer to address your envelopes. You only have to type the list once, and you can use it over and over again.

7. Manage your personal finances.

Personal financial management programs can balance your checkbook and automatically print checks to pay your monthly bills. You can also pay your bills by direct electronic transfer, all managed from your computer. If you want to play with the high rollers, you can tie into the stock exchange ticker just like the pros.

8. Become a publisher.

A computer and a laser printer are all you need to start your own newsletter, magazine, or book publishing operation. Many of the books and magazines you see every day are produced with the same tools you can put on your desktop and operate yourself. Take your laser-printed master pages to a commercial print shop, and you're in business.

9. Keep the kids out of your hair.

Why spend your money on Nintendo games when you can buy a computer that lets you do something useful as well as have fun flying airplanes, experiencing cliff-hanging adventures, and

fighting space invaders. Who knows, the kids might even find that doing something productive on the computer is more fun than racing at Le Mans.

10. **Prowl for information on CompuServe.**

Electronic bulletin boards are treasure troves of information. You can find answers to almost any question, find interest groups for just about any interest, send electronic mail, and carry on stimulating dialogues with people in places you've never heard of before. All you need is a modem and a phone line.

11. **Harass your congressperson.**

China's democracy movement was fueled by faxes—yours can be too. The next time your senator deserves a pat on the back or a kick in the rump, don't waste money on old-fashioned telegrams. Send a fax with some typographic impact.

12. **Browse the encyclopedia.**

Whole reference works are available on CD—*Grolier's Encyclopedia* and the complete works of Shakespeare, for instance. And since disks are cheaper than books, these resources are much cheaper on CD than in printed form.

I HATE

The Buzzword Glossary

8-bit color This color display scheme dedicates one byte (8 bits) of information to describe each pixel of the image. An 8-bit display, then, can show 256 different colors on the screen at any one time. Compare to *24-bit color*.

24-bit color A color technology that uses 3 bytes (24 bits) of information to describe the color of each pixel on a computer screen or each dot of a bitmapped image. The three-byte description is capable of representing 16.7 million colors. Compare to *8-bit color*.

access time The time, measured in milliseconds (ms), a hard-disk drive takes to find and record information. An access time of less than 15 milliseconds is considered very fast. Compare to *seek time*.

add-on board A printed-circuit board that plugs into a slot inside the computer and controls something the computer does (such as show the video image) or adds a new capability (such as scanner control or added communication ports). Also called an *expansion card*.

AppleTalk The networking standard used by Apple Macintosh computers to communicate with other Macintoshes. Also available for PCs, using special software and an add-on card.

application program A computer program for doing a particular task, such as word processing, creating graphics, or playing games.

ASIC Application-Specific Integrated Circuit, a chip that enhances the performance of a particular task, such as printing or creating graphic images. Pronounced *A-sick*.

ASCII American Standard for Computer Information Interchange, a communications standard that assigns specific numbers to the letters, numbers, and symbols found on a computer keyboard. All computers can read information saved in ASCII format. Pronounced *AS-key*.

aspect ratio   The ratio of height to width of a *pixel* on a computer screen. Most current monitors feature a 1:1 aspect ratio, which translates into a square pixel. See *pixel*.

asynchronous   In communications between computers, a transfer of information that does not rely on both computers running at the same speed.

AT   This IBM trade name stands for "Advanced Technology" and refers to a class of PCs built around the Intel 80286 microprocessor. They're no longer considered to be at all advanced.

background processing   Work done by a computer (such as printing a file) that is carried out behind the scenes while you continue working uninterrupted in your application program. Because the work you're doing in your application does not take up all of the computer's time, it can use its idle moments to perform the background processing. Compare to *multitasking*.

back-lit screen   In laptop computers, a type of LCD screen in which the light source is directly behind the screen image. Compare to *side-lit screen*.

baud rate   The rate at which a modem transfers information across a telephone line. 2400 baud is the standard rate for modems.

benchmark   A laboratory standard by which the performance of computers, computer components, and application programs are compared. Benchmarks attempt to imitate real-life situations, but they're not accurate predictors of the performance you'll actually experience with your computer.

Bernoulli drive   A high-capacity disk drive that uses removable disk cartridges that resemble large floppy disks. These disks have capacities of 40 megabytes or more.

binary   Describes information that is stored as a series of on/off signals typically represented by the numbers 1 and 0. All computer information is stored and transmitted in binary form. You can use the word *digital* synonymously in this context.

BIOS   Basic Input/Output System, the software that is permanently recorded in chips inside the computer. BIOS (pronounced *BY-oss*) controls the transfer of information between the various hardware elements of the computer.

bit   The basic unit of computer information, representing a single *binary* decision (see *binary*), which—like an electrical switch—represents on or off, represented digitally by the numbers 1 and 0. See also *byte*.

bit map   A graphic image constructed on a checkerboard-like grid. A script written by a program dictates which of the squares in the grid are colored in and which are left blank. A bitmapped image, then, is a record of precisely where each dot should be placed on a particular grid. A bitmapped image is tied to a particular resolution, which defines the size of the squares on the grid. See also *object-oriented graphics* and *raster image processor*.

bitmapped font   A set of letters, numbers, and symbols that has been drawn dot-by-dot—*bitmapped*—for a particular size and resolution. For best results, only use bitmapped fonts at the size and resolution for which they were drawn.

bomb   A program failure from which there is no recovery except to shut down the program and start over again. If the bomb involves the operating system, you must turn off the computer and restart it. Also used as a verb.

boot   To start a computer and its operating system. You *boot* every time you turn on or reset the computer.

boot disk   The disk in a computer on which the operating system is stored (typically a hard disk).

bps   Bits per second, the measure of how fast information is passed from computer to computer.

bubble jet   A printing technology (related to the *inkjet*) in which marks are made by a tiny nozzle that forms and bursts a minuscule bubble of ink onto the paper.

buffer   An area of a computer's memory where information is temporarily stored until it can be used. For example, when one computer sends information faster than the receiving computer can handle it, the incoming information is *buffered* in memory until the receiving computer can handle it.

bundle   A computer sales term referring to several things that are packaged together. When you buy a computer, software may be *bundled* with it.

bus   The system of electronic pathways within a computer that link the main components together. Different computers use different buses, the difference often being how much data can pass along the bus at one time. This data capacity is referred to as the *width* of the bus and is measured in the number of bits that the bus can pass along simultaneously. There are 8- 16- and 32-bit buses. See also *EISA, ISA, local bus,* and *Micro Channel Architecture.*

bus mouse   A mouse that is connected directly to the main circuitry of the computer. Compare to *serial mouse*.

byte   A unit of computer information that consists of 8 bits read together as a single "word." Bytes are used to measure the size of a computer's memory, the capacity of hard disks, and the size of computer files.

cache   An area of memory where information is stored for later or repeated use. A memory cache is used to speed up computer performance.

CDEV   On the Macintosh, a program or utility that appears in the Control Panel. Short for Control panel DEVice. Pronounced *SEE-dev*.

CD-ROM   A compact disc (like the ones used for music) that contains computer programs or files. They're called ROMs because they can only be read, not erased or recorded on. See also *read-only memory*.

central processing unit   The main box of a computer, which contains the microprocessor, bus, and disk drives.

Centronics   The most common standard for parallel communications.

CGA   Color Graphics Adapter, a 4-color computer display standard popularized by IBM in its PC-AT personal computers. Very uncool, old technology.

clock doubling   A technique for doubling the speed at which a microprocessor can handle information. It can be used on DX series 80386 and 80486 chips used in PC compatibles. *Clock doubling* does not affect the speed at which information travels across the bus of the computer—it only affects the speed of processing within the microprocessor. See also *clock speed* and DX.

clock speed   The speed of a computer's internal metronome, which paces all of the microprocessor's activities. Instructions and computing events are timed to happen precisely at the tick of the clock. The faster the clock speed, then, the faster the computer can run. Common clock speeds for PCs (in megahertz) are 16, 20, 25, 33, 50 and 66. The higher the clock speed is, the better.

clone   Any PC not built by IBM. A clone isn't a bad thing—many of the best PCs are built by companies other than IBM.

communications ports   Sockets in a computer through which information is sent to or received from other devices, such as other computers, modems, or printers.

compatible   Two pieces of hardware or software that work together are called *compatible*. When they're 100% compatible they work together under all circumstances. Not all things that claim to be compatible are 100% compatible. See also *downward compatibility* and *upward compatibility*.

console model   A personal computer whose CPU is horizontal and sits on the desktop, often with the monitor on top of it. Compare to *tower*.

coprocessor   A chip that speeds up a computer by assisting the main microprocessor in performing specific tasks. The most common ones are math coprocessors and graphics coprocessors.

cps   Characters per second, a speed rating for impact printers and raster image processors. See also *raster image processors*.

CPU   See *central processing unit*.

crash   The failure of a hard disk, usually for mechanical reasons.

CRT   Short for Cathode Ray Tube, the picture tube in a computer monitor, essentially like that in a TV set. This term is rarely used; most people just refer to the whole thing as a monitor or screen.

DA   See *desk accessory*.

daisywheel printer   An impact printer that prints characters in a manner similar to a typewriter. Nobody uses these anymore, with good reason. Daisywheel printers are agonizingly slow and about as quiet as an outboard motor.

data   A fancy way to say information.

data path   The information pipeline that leads in and out of a computer's microprocessor. This path is measured in terms of how many bits can pass through it simultaneously.

daughterboard   A small add-on board that is mounted onto a larger add-on board.

default   A pre-established hardware or software setting in a computer or program. A default setting defines the way a computer or program behaves unless you tell it to do otherwise.

de-Gauss   To remove an accumulated static electrical charge from a color computer monitor. Over time, excess charges build up in the monitor that can distort colors. Pressing the monitor's de-Gaussing button discharges this build-up. *Gauss* rhymes with *mouse*.

desk accessory   On a Macintosh, a memory-resident program found under the Apple menu. Also called a *DA*. See also *memory-resident program*.

desktop publishing   A computer application that combines text and graphics on the same page for printing completely laid-out pages.

dialog box   In some programs, an on-screen fill-in-the-blanks form in which you issue a number of commands at one time.

digital   Refers to information stored in a computer as a series of numbers, usually 1's and 0's. See also *binary*.

DIN connector   A kind of computer cable connection used for modems, mice, and other devices. DIN stands for Deutsche Industrie Norm, a German standard.

dip switches   Tiny switches used to set up computer hardware components to work together. They're typically found on printers and add-on boards. With any luck, you'll never have to mess with dip switches. They're better left to professionals.

diskette   A thin plastic disk with a magnetic coating used for recording computer information. The disks, which are mounted in a rigid housing, are inserted into a reader/recorder built into the computer. Also called a *floppy disk*. See also *disk drive*.

disk cache   A part of a computer's memory used to speed the transfer of information to and from a hard disk. See also *cache*.

disk drive   A device built into a computer for recording and reading information to and from diskettes. The drives record and replay information in a manner similar to that used in a cassette tape recorder. Also called a floppy disk drive to distinguish it from a hard disk drive. See also *hard disk*.

display   What you see on a computer's monitor. Sometimes this term is also used synonymously with *monitor*. It's also sometimes used to refer to the monitor/display adapter combination.

display adapter   An add-on board inside a computer that controls the image displayed on the monitor. A single display adapter usually works with a number of monitors and may support a number of display standards.

display standard   A specific industry accepted way of displaying images on a computer screen. A display standard defines how many colors are displayed, the resolution of the screen, and the shape of the pixels used to create the image. See CGA, EGA, *QuickDraw, super* VGA, and VGA.

DOS   Disk Operating System, the operating system used by PC compatible computers. Rhymes with moss. See also *MS-DOS*.

dot-matrix printer   An impact printer that builds images from dots created by an array of rods that strike the paper through an inked ribbon. These rods are driven in patterns against the paper. These patterns can be used to print text or graphic images.

dot pitch   The distance between pixels on a computer monitor.

double density   Refers to a diskette that can hold approximately 700-800 kilobytes of information.

double sided   See *double density*.

download   To send information from a bigger computer to a smaller one. For example, files can be downloaded to a printer. Likewise, when you connect your computer to a larger computer and draw information from it, you are downloading that information. See also *upload*.

downloadable fonts   Collections of letters, numbers, and symbols that can be sent from a computer to be stored in the memory of a printer in order to speed up printing.

downward compatibility   This term refers to a new product—hardware or software— that also works with older or less powerful equipment or programs. Also called backward compatibility.

dpi   Dots per inch, a measure of printer resolution. More dots per inch mean a smoother and clearer printed image.

draft quality   Describes the quality of low-resolution dot-matrix type. This quality is not considered good enough for business correspondence. See also *near-letter quality*.

DRAM   Pronounced *DEE-ram*. See *dynamic RAM*.

draw graphics   See *object-oriented graphics*.

driver   A software program that an application program or operating system uses to work with a particular piece of hardware, such as a printer or monitor. The driver translates instructions from the program into a language that the device can understand.

dye sublimation printing   An expensive color desktop printing technique that uses dyes to paint the printed page.

dynamic RAM   Memory that fades if not recharged continuously. Compare to *static RAM*.

DX   A suffix added to the numerical names of 80386 and 80486 (e.g., 80486DX) microprocessor chips that can include built-in math coprocessors and are capable of having the clock speeds doubled. See also *coprocessor*.

DX2   A suffix added to the numerical names of certain 80386 and 80486 chips to indicate that they use technology that doubles their internal clock speed. See also *clock doubling* and *DX*.

edge-lit screen   See *side-lit display*.

EGA   Enhanced Graphics Adapter, an IBM display standard for PCs that is the successor to CGA. It features 16 colors and 640-by-350-pixel resolution.

EISA   Extended Industry Standard Architecture, a PC computer bus standard that allows 32-bits to pass simultaneously. See also *bus*, *ISA*, *local bus*, and *Micro Channel Architecture*.

emulation   A software technique that allows one program to act like another one without violating software copyrights. This term is used most commonly in reference to printers, which can emulate the printing technology of their competitors.

EPROM   Erasable Programmable Read-Only Memory, pronounced *E-prom*. This term refers to ROM chips that can be re-programmed with new instructions. In PCs, EPROMs hold information about the hardware setup of the computer so the operating system knows what it's dealing with. Also called *EEPROMs* (for Electrically Erasable...).

end user   You, the person doing all the work.

ESDI   Enhanced Small Device Interface, a high-speed connection between a hard disk and the microprocessor of a computer.

expansion card   See *add-on board*.

expansion slot   A socket in the main circuit board of the computer into which you plug add-on boards. See also *add-on board*.

fax machine   Short for *facsimile machine*. A fax machine records a digital image of a printed page that can be transmitted to and printed by another fax machine. The resolution of faxes following current international standards is 200 dots per inch. See also *fax modem*.

fax modem   A modem that can also transmit fax images of documents you create on your computer. Whereas a typical fax machine sends an image of a paper original over the phone lines, a fax modem creates the facsimile image directly from an electronic computer file. See also *modem*.

file   The form in which a program saves information on a disk. A *file* can be a text document, a graphic image, a spreadsheet, and so on.

file server   On a network, a computer used as shared file storage by all the other computers.

firmware   Software that has been written permanently into computer chips (ROM).

fixed disk   See *hard disk*.

FLOP   FLoating-point OPeration, a kind of mathematical calculation

done by a computer. Operating speeds of computers are sometimes expressed in megaFLOPs (MFLOPs). Pronounced *flop* and *M-flop*.

floppy disk　See *diskette*.

font　In computer text composition, a program used to store a *typeface*, which is a collection of letters, numbers, and symbols in a particular design. See also *bitmapped font* and *outline font*.

footprint　Refers to the amount of space a computer takes up on a desk.

font cartridge　In certain printers, a plug-in cartridge that contains typefaces in various designs stored permanently in memory chips.

format (verb)—To prepare a diskette for use by a particular computer. Formatting divides the diskette into filing zones called *sectors*. Macintoshes and PCs format diskettes differently, even though both can use 3.5" diskettes.

format (noun)—The way a computer file or program is recorded or written. For a particular program to be able to read a file, the file must be written in a *format* that the program can understand. Likewise, a program such as a font must be written in a format that works with the printer with which it will be used.

function key　An auxiliary key (marked F1, F2, and so on) on a computer keyboard used to issue program commands. You can also program function keys to perform various complex tasks at a single keystroke. See also *macro*.

GB　See *gigabyte*.

gigabyte　One billion bytes, or 1,000 megabytes. Pronounced *Gig-UH-bite*.

graphical user interface   A pictorial way of displaying a program to a user that makes the program easier to understand and to use. Files and programs are represented on screen by images called *icons*. Program commands are organized into *menus*; you can execute various actions by selecting the desired option from the various menus the program offers.

graphics coprocessor   See *coprocessor*.

grayscale   The range of shades of gray between black and white as represented on a computer screen or in a printed image.

GUI   See *graphical user interface*.

half-height drive   A compact hard-disk drive that takes up only half the vertical space inside a computer that a normal hard-disk drive occupies. This drive leaves room for other things in your computer.

hard card   A *hard disk* built onto an add-on board for easy installation inside a computer. Hard cards have limited capacities and are slower than regular hard-disk drives.

hard disk   A rigid magnetic disk used for storing information inside a computer. Hard disks hold much more information than *diskettes* and are typically mounted permanently inside a computer. A single hard-disk drive can contain several disks—or *platters*—for even larger storage capacities.

hardware   The electronic and mechanical parts of a computer. Compare to *software*.

hertz   A measure of frequency equal to one cycle per second. It is used to measure the speed at which a computer's display adapter draws the images on a computer's screen. In multiples of 1000 (*megahertz*, or MHz), it is used to measure the clock speed of a computer. See also *clock speed*, *display adapter*, and *refresh rate*.

high-density   Refers to diskettes that can contain over one megabyte of information.

Hz   See *hertz*.

icon   A graphic representation of a program, file, or process on a computer's screen.

IDE   Integrated Device Electronics, a standard for computer hardware communication, used as a designation for high-speed hard-disk drives.

INIT   On the Macintosh, a program that loads itself into memory when you start up the computer (short for initialization file). Pronounced *in-IT*.

inkjet   A printing technology that uses a nozzle (or series of nozzles for color) to spray ink onto the page. The bursts of spray are very tiny and are analogous to the dots created by a laser printer.

input/output   Refers to the computer receiving information from an outside source, or sending information out to one. Often shortened to I/O.

interface   (1) The view of a program presented on the screen of a computer and the methods used to operate the program. (2) The connection between two computer devices, such as a computer and a printer. Serial and parallel connections are also called *interfaces*.

interlacing   A technique used for drawing images on a computer screen. The image on a computer screen is drawn as a series of horizontal lines, and the image is constantly being redrawn to keep the screen illuminated. The screen is redrawn dozens of times per second. In an interlaced screen, only every other line is drawn each time the screen image is refreshed, which makes the display adapter less expensive to manufacture because it has to do less work during each refresh cycle.

Interlaced screens have a tendency to flicker, as the newly refreshed lines contrast with the alternating ones that are beginning to fade out. See also *refresh rate*.

I/O   See *input/output*.

ISA   Industry Standard Architecture, a bus design used in many PC computers and introduced by the IBM PC-AT. The ISA bus can pass 16-bits simultaneously. See also *bus*, *EISA*, and *Micro Channel Architecture*.

jumper   A switch-like setting on some add-on boards that must be adjusted to make them work with particular hardware.

K   See *kilobyte*.

kilobyte   A measure of computer storage capacity equal to 1,000 bytes, or about 175 average-length English words.

LAN   Pronounced *lan*. See *local area network*.

landscape   The horizontal orientation of a printed page, so that lines of text run the length of the printed sheet instead of across its width. Compare to *portrait*.

language   A standard way of instructing a computer how to perform specific tasks. Like a human language, computer programming languages use words—actual combinations of letters—to represent both simple and complex sets of instructions for the computer to follow. See also *page description language*.

laser printer   A high-resolution printer that uses a laser beam to draw the image of the printed page. These printers give the best image of all affordable printers, but cost considerably more than dot-matrix and inkjet printers.

LCD   Liquid Crystal Display, a technology that creates images by making areas of an opaque surface selectively transparent, allowing light from behind to project through. LCD technology is used for screen displays on laptop computers and for some types of high-resolution printers.

LCS   Liquid Crystal Shutter. See *LCD*.

LED printer   Light Emitting Diode printers use an array of tiny lights that act in place of a laser to draw page images that are printed using a technology similar to photocopiers. Compare to *laser printer*.

letter-quality   Type created on a computer printer that is deemed of acceptable quality for business correspondence.

local area network   A series of connections linking a number of computers, as well as shared printers and other devices. Most local area networks are in a single office or building and have at their center a *file server*, a computer that is used solely as a storage center and not as a workstation. Novell Netware is a well-known local-area network program.

local bus   A high-speed detour around a PC computer's standard bus. This link creates a direct connection between the microprocessor and the computer's display adapter and hard-disk drive, which speeds up the performance of both.

LocalTalk   The communication and wiring standard used by Apple Macintosh computers to communicate with other hardware devices, such as printers.

MCA   See *Micro Channel Architecture*.

macro   A computer shorthand expression—typically a single keystroke—that represents a series of keystrokes and/or program commands. Macros are typically assigned to one of the function keys.

math coprocessor   See *coprocessor*.

megabyte   A measure of computer storage equal to 1,000 kilobytes. See also *byte* and *kilobyte*.

megahertz   1,000 hertz, or 1,000 cycles per second. A unit used to measure the clock speed of a microprocessor. Abbreviated MHz. Common megahertz ratings for 386 and 486 PCs are 16, 20, 25, 33, 50 and 66.

memory   In a computer, an array of electrical charges stored in special chips used for temporary information storage. See also *dynamic RAM*, *RAM*, *static RAM*, and *video RAM*.

memory hog   An application program that requires a lot of memory to operate efficiently.

memory-resident programs   Application programs that, once started, remain active in memory and can be operated simultaneously with another program. Examples of these are calendar and phone book programs that you can consult while you run your word processor. On PCs, these programs are called *TSRs*, which stand for Terminate and Stay Resident. On the Macintosh, these programs are called *desk accessories*.

menu   In an application program, a list of commands or options. In a menu-driven program, all the possible commands you can issue to a program are organized logically into a series of menus, making the commands easier to use.

MFM   Modified Frequency Modulation, a slow, out-of-date standard for the transfer of information from hard disk to microprocessor.

MHz   See *megahertz*.

Micro Channel Architecture   A superior high-speed PC bus standard proposed by IBM but rejected by most PC manufacturers.

microprocessor   The chip that acts as the brain of a personal computer. The power of a computer is based on the speed with which its microprocessor can handle information.

MIDI   Musical Instrument Device Interface, a connection that links special digital musical instruments to a personal computer.

millisecond   One thousandth of a second, abbreviated *ms* or *msec*. A hard disk drive's access time is measured in milliseconds.

MIPS   Millions of Instructions Per Second, a measure of computer processing speed.

MDA   Monochrome Display Adapter, the original one-color-on-black monitor standard used on IBM PCs and compatibles. See also CGA, EGA, *super VGA,* and *VGA.*

modem   A device that allows a computer to send or receive information via telephone lines. A modem translates the digital information used by a computer into the analog form used by telephones. (The word *modem* comes from a reference to this MOdulation-DEModulation process.) See also *fax modem.*

monitor   The TV-like screen of a computer.

monochrome   Describes a monitor that displays one color in addition to the background color of the screen. Originally, this term referred to green on black, but now it commonly refers to black on white, or vice versa.

monospacing   A printing standard in which all the letters of an alphabet take up the same amount of horizontal space on a line, as with manual typewriters. Compare to *proportional spacing.*

motherboard The main circuit board inside a computer to which all other parts attach. The microprocessor is attached to the motherboard.

mouse A hand-held pointing device used to issue program commands, manipulate information on the screen, and draw images in graphics programs.

ms See *millisecond*.

MS-DOS Abbreviation for Microsoft Disk Operating System. *DOS* was originally manufactured by both IBM and Microsoft Corporation. Pronounced *EMM-ess-doss*.

multimedia Computer technology that combines text, sounds, and moving and still video images into a single presentation.

multisync Describes a monitor that can operate under several video display standards.

multitasking An advanced computer capability in which the microprocessor can perform several tasks simultaneously without the tasks affecting one another. In effect, the microprocessor divides itself into parts and assigns each part to one of the tasks. Compare this concept to *background processing* in which the computer appears to be doing two things at once but is actually dividing its time between the two tasks, which causes both to occur more slowly.

nanoseconds Millionths of a second, used to describe the speed of RAM chips.

near-letter quality A description of dot-matrix printer type that may be better than draft quality, but which is not good enough for typical business correspondence.

network A series of computers connected together for the purpose of sharing information or processing power. The computers in a network

need not be physically wired together. See also *local area network* and *wide area network*.

network interface card   An add-on card that adapts a computer to communicate over a network.

NIC   See *network interface card*.

non-interlaced   A computer monitor that completely redraws the image during each refresh cycle. Non-interlaced monitors are better than interlaced monitors. See also *refresh rate* and *interlacing*.

non-volatile memory   Computer memory supported by batteries so that it doesn't evaporate in case of power outages. Laptop computers often use non-volatile memory that relies on secondary batteries to protect against failure of the main battery pack.

ns   See *nanoseconds*.

object-oriented graphics   Graphic images that are described as a series of mathematical equations. One advantage of object—or draw—graphics is that they can be scaled to a different size without loss of clarity by mathematically manipulating the equations that describe them.

Bitmapped graphics, by comparison, cannot be scaled well because they're composed of a specific arrangement of dots. Scaling such an image down in size necessitates getting rid of some dots; making it larger calls upon the computer to add dots. In either case, the image inevitably becomes distorted.

Object-oriented graphics are sometimes simply called *object graphics* or *vector graphics*. See also *bit map*.

OCR   See *optical character recognition*.

OEM   Original Equipment Manufacturer. OEMs are the manufacturers of computer equipment that other companies eventually put their names on.

on-site service   A condition of a computer warranty that specifies that the manufacturer or his agent will come to your home or office to do repairs.

operating system   The program that coordinates the activities of a computer's hardware and provides filing and basic communication services. Application programs cannot run unless the operating system has been turned on and is functioning properly.

optical character recognition   A software technology that allows a computer to decipher text based on images of printed pages. Typically an image of a page is captured by a scanner and the optical character recognition software analyzes the shapes of the character images and converts the scanned page image into an editable computer text file.

optical media   Storage systems such as compact discs, which use a laser beam to record information.

outline font   A program consisting of a collection of letters, numbers, and symbols whose shapes (outlines) are stored as mathematical equations. With an *outline font*, you can scale the letters to any size without distortion and print them at any resolution. See also *bitmapped font*, *object-oriented graphics*, and *raster image processor*.

OS/2   A powerful PC operating system created by IBM with a graphic user interface similar to Microsoft Windows. See also *operating system* and *Windows*.

page description language   A programming language used to describe the ways in which a page can be printed. It can instruct a printer to create images consisting of bitmapped graphics, object-oriented graphics, type, and color. See also *PCL*, *PostScript*, and *QuickDraw*.

parallel   A high-speed communications link consisting of several *parallel* channels, used primarily to connect PCs and printers. See also *Centronics*.

PC   A generic name for personal computers based on the original IBM design and built around the Intel series of 80xxx microprocessors (8086, 8088, 80286, etc.).

PCL   Printer Command Language, a page description language created by Hewlett-Packard for use in their printers.

PDL   See *page description language*.

pel   See *pixel*.

pen-based computing   A technology that uses a pen-like stylus instead of a keyboard or mouse for introducing information into a computer or issuing program commands.

peripherals   Hardware devices that can be added to a computer, such as a printer, modem, or scanner.

pixel   Abbreviation for picture element, one of the dots used to create images on a computer screen.

platform   A generic word for *computer*, used for clarity in contexts where incompatible computers are being discussed or compared. Software that runs on several *platforms*, for example, is software that runs on different types of computers, such as PCs, Macintoshes, and mainframe computers.

plotter   A printer that creates line images with a pen. The pen is mounted on a track that moves side to side while the paper is moved backward and forward beneath this track, allowing lines of all angles and curves to be reproduced. Plotters are used for drafting and engineering applications, or where very large printouts are needed.

populate   To fill a computer board with chips, usually memory chips. A board that is filled to capacity is said to be *fully populated*.

port (noun)—A plug on a computer through which information enters or leaves. See *AppleTalk*, *parallel*, and *serial*.

port (verb)— To translate an application program created for one kind of computer so that it will work with another kind. For example, you can *port* a Macintosh program to the PC, and vice versa.

portrait   The normal vertical orientation of a printed page, in which lines of text run the width of the printed sheet, as in a typical letter. Compare to *landscape*.

PostScript   A page description language created by Adobe Systems. PostScript has its own font format of the same name. See also *page description language* and *raster image processor*.

ppi   Pixels per inch, a measure of resolution for computer monitors.

ppm   Pages per minute, a measure of the maximum speed at which a printer can operate.

power supply   A transformer that passes power to the components of a computer. The more add-on boards a computer contains, the larger the power supply it needs.

processing   A catch-all term that describes the handling of information by a computer. In general, processing involves changing information from one form into a new and more useful form. Examples include converting numbers into a financial record, changing simple typed words into a newsletter page, or turning instructions to a program into visual images on the computer's screen.

proportional spacing   A printing system in which the letters of an alphabet have varying widths; an i, for instance, takes up less space on a line than an m. Compare to *monospacing*.

proprietary   Refers to a non-standard technology that is specific to one manufacturer and is typically protected by patent or copyright. Macintosh hardware, for example, is based on a proprietary design; it can only be manufactured by Apple Computer. The design of a PC-compatible is not proprietary, so it can be used by many manufacturers.

protocol   A set of technological specifications devised to ensure compatibility between two computers or pieces of computer hardware. The word is used most commonly in regard to telecommunications (telephone connections) between computers.

QuickDraw   A page description language used by Apple Macintoshes primarily to create screen images. It can also be used to drive a printer. See also *page description language*.

RAM   See *random-access memory*.

random-access memory   RAM, the principle kind of computer memory used for temporary information storage. It's called random access because a computer doesn't have to read from the beginning to the end of the storage area to find a piece of information.

raster image processor   A program or hardware device that takes instructions written in a page description language and translates them into page images consisting of the dots that laser printers (and other similar printers) use to print pages. See also *page description language*.

read-only memory   Computer chips that contain permanently recorded program instructions. Usually abbreviated as *ROM*.

refresh rate   The speed at which a monitor redraws the image on a computer screen, which typically occurs 60 to 80 times per second. Each redrawing of the screen is called a *cycle*, so the refresh rate is measured in cycles per second, or hertz. See also *interlacing*.

resident fonts   Collections of letters, numbers, and symbols that are built into a printer, typically in read-only memory (ROM) chips. Compare to *downloadable fonts*.

resolution   In devices that make images composed of dots (such as monitors and laser printers), the number of dots per inch that the device can create.

RGB   Red, Green, Blue, refers to the three basic colors used by color monitors to create all other colors.

RIP   See *raster image processor*.

rigid disk   See *hard disk*.

ROM   See *read-only memory*.

RS-232   A name for the most popular PC serial communication standard, as well as the connection and cable it uses.

save   To permanently record computer information, usually on a hard disk or diskette.

scanner   A device that records images from a printed page or piece of photographic film and converts them into a digital form that a computer can use.

scalable fonts   See *outline font*.

SCSI   Small Computer Systems Interface, a high speed communications connection for linking devices such as scanners and hard-disk drives to a computer. Pronounced *scuzzy*. Honestly.

sectors   Areas on a hard disk or diskette in which a computer program stores information. The size and arrangement of the sectors are defined by the operating system during a process called formatting.

seek time   The time it takes a hard disk drive to locate a piece of information stored on its disk. Compare to *access time*.

serial   A communications connection that sends bits of information individually and sequentially. It is commonly used for modem connections. Compare to *parallel*.

serial mouse   A hand-held pointing device that attaches to the computer by means of a serial connection.

shadow RAM   A special area of computer memory into which the computer's BIOS is copied for faster computer operation.

shell program   A program that metaphorically sits over the top of another program and changes the way it operates or the way in which you interact with it. The most common kind of shell program is used to make DOS easier to work with.

side-lit display   In laptop computers, a form of LCD display in which the pixels are illuminated from the edges of the screen. This kind of display generally results in a dimmer display than one produced by a back-lit display.

SIMMs   Single In-line Memory Modules, sets of memory chips (RAM) that plug into sockets inside a computer. See also *memory* and *RAM*.

slots   See *expansion slot*.

soft font   A name given to PC software fonts that can be stored in the memory of a printer. The name distinguishes them from ROM-based fonts used in some printers. See also *font*.

software   The programs used on a computer.

SRAM   See *static RAM*.

standard   An industry-accepted way of doing something. Hardware standards, for example, assure that computer parts will work together. There are software standards for creating files in ways that allow them to be used by many different application programs.

static RAM   A kind of memory chip that holds information without having to be electrically refreshed from time to time, making it faster and more expensive than dynamic RAM. See also *memory* and *RAM*.

storage device   Any piece of computer hardware used for permanent storage of information, such as hard disk drives.

supertwist   The leading kind of liquid-crystal display used in laptop computers.

super VGA   An extension of the normal VGA display standard for PCs that expands screen resolution to 800 by 600 pixels or to 1024 by 768 pixels.

SX   A suffix added to the numerical names of certain 80386 and 80486 (e.g., 80486SX) to differentiate them from the potentially more powerful DX chips. See also *DX* and *clock doubling*.

system board   See *motherboard*.

telecommunicate   To pass information between computers using telephone lines.

terminate-and-stay-resident programs   See *memory-resident programs*.

thermal printers   Printers that use a special heat-sensitive paper for printing.

thermal transfer printing   A color printing technology that uses heat to transfer color from special ribbons to the printed page. Also called *wax transfer printing*.

tower   A personal computer whose CPU is vertical and designed to stand on the floor. Compare to *console model*.

TSR   Terminate and Stay Resident, another name for *memory-resident programs*.

trackball   A pointing device similar to a mouse that consists of a ball, which you rotate with the palm of your hand to cause the cursor to move on-screen.

transfer rate   The speed at which a hard disk can transfer information to the microprocessor.

TrueImage   A PostScript clone made by Microsoft Corporation.

TrueType   An outline font format used by Macintosh computers and Microsoft Windows.

turbo   A non-specific marketing term that indicates enhanced speed or performance.

typeface   A collection of letters, numbers, and symbols that share a specific design. Compare to *font*.

upload   To send information from a smaller computer to a larger one. Compare to *download*.

upward compatibility   This term refers to an older product—hardware or software—that continues to work with a new generation of more powerful equipment or programs.

user-friendly   Refers to a program that is easy to use, but in particular easy to learn. Most computers are neither friendly nor unfriendly; the programs that run on them are what make them hard or easy to use.

vector graphics   See *object-oriented graphics*.

VESA bus A local bus standard proposed by the Video Electronics Standards Association and accepted by major hardware and software vendors.

VGA Video Graphics Adapter, a PC display standard created by IBM that offers a resolution of 640 by 480 pixels in 16 colors. VGA is the standard display on PC-compatible computers.

video adapter See *display adapter*.

video RAM Memory in which a display adapter constructs screen images before they're sent to the monitor to be displayed. The more colors or grays you want to see on-screen, the more video RAM the display adapter needs.

virtual In computers, a word used to describe something that functions as if it's something else. For instance, a *virtual disk drive* is not a mechanical device; it's a part of the computer's memory manipulated to act as if it were a disk drive—you can save files there, copy things to and from it, and so on. See also *virtual memory*.

virtual memory A technology that uses hard disk storage space as if it were part of the computer's RAM. Virtual memory isn't as fast as true RAM, but it can effectively enlarge the memory capacity of a computer without having to add any new memory chips to the machine.

virus A small program designed to invade a computer and be passed along to other computers with which it communicates. Computer viruses can spread by infected diskettes or by direct computer-to-computer connections on a network or over telephone lines. Most viruses are destructive in some way, destroying data or interfering with the operation of the computer.

VM See *virtual memory*.

I HATE BUYING A COMPUTER!

volatile memory   Memory that is erased as soon as the power to it is cut off. Compare to *non-volatile memory*.

VRAM   See *video RAM*.

wait state   A pause in the microprocessor's activity while it awaits information to arrive from the computer's memory. Zero-wait-state computers have the speed of the RAM chips coordinated with the microprocessor's clock speed to eliminate these pauses.

WAN   See *wide area network*.

wax transfer printing   See *thermal transfer printing*.

wide area network   A series of computers that are connected over a large distance, usually by telephone lines or satellite connections.

window   A rectangular work space on a computer's screen in which a program operates. Several windows, each representing an individual file or a separate program, can be open and visible on the screen at one time.

Windows   An extension to the DOS operating system for PCs created by Microsoft Corporation. Also called *Microsoft Windows* or *MS Windows*.

write-black   Some laser printers use the laser to strike the shapes of letters and other things that will print on the page. These printers are called *write-black printers*. The laser beam tends to splatter a little when it hits the surface of the toner drum, which causes the letters of write black-printers to spread out just a bit. Compare to *write-white*.

write-white   Laser printers that use the laser to strike everywhere *but* the areas that are supposed to print. Because the laser beam tends to splatter a little bit when it hits the toner drum, the letters of write-white printers tend to be slightly eroded around the edges, making them appear slightly thinner on the page. Compare to *write-black*.

WYSIWYG What You See Is What You Get, a term that refers to a computer display in which what you see on-screen faithfully represents what your final printed page will look like.

XT An IBM trademark for computers based on the Intel 8086 micro-processor. IBM-XTs were the first PCs to use a hard disk. These computers are hopelessly outdated. If someone tries to sell you one, walk out of the showroom in a huff.

I HATE

Index